TREASURES
IN THE DARK

TREASURES
IN THE DARK

90 REFLECTIONS ON FINDING BRIGHT
HOPE HIDDEN IN THE HURTING

BY KATHERINE WOLF

WITH ALEX WOLF

W Publishing Group

.N Imprint of Thomas Nelson

ISBN 978-1-4003-3821-4 (HC)
ISBN 978-1-4003-3823-8 (eBook)
ISBN 978-1-4003-3824-5 (audiobook)

Library of Congress Control Number: 2023947112

Printed in the United States of America

24 25 26 27 28 LBC 5 4 3 2 1

CONTENTS

PART TWO

FOR THE HEALING: *Befriending the Lives We Have*

PART THREE
FOR THE HOPING: *Finding Our Lives in the Bigger Story*

INTRODUCTION

I f you've spent more than twenty-four hours on earth, you've probably figured out that this place can be just a little dark. And sometimes, pitch-black. As far as I can tell, not a single one of us signed up for this whole "being born" deal. I don't know about you, but I never received a cosmic consent form or liability waiver. If one of those did exist, I imagine it would open with a big, bold disclaimer: "Warning! This is gonna hurt! Proceed at your own risk."

If you are of the Christian tradition like I am, then you know our shared faith doesn't shy away from acknowledging the dark stuff. In fact, the first few sentences of the Bible tell us that God carved the world out of a formless, empty void. Ages and ages later, Jesus reiterated the same idea without mincing any words: "Here on earth you will have many trials and sorrows" (John 16:33 NLT). Hey, you can't say He didn't warn us!

The very raw material of reality is darkness. So why are we taken by total surprise when suffering and sorrow find us?

For a while, I wasn't so much afraid of the dark as I was altogether and blissfully unaware of it. Then I suffered a catastrophic brain stem stroke when I was twenty-six years old. Until that point, my life had been largely *pain-free* in a way I had mistaken for *blessed*. I was born into and raised by a loving and financially stable family who sent me off to a small Christian university. There I met my now husband, Jay. And shortly after our blowout country-club wedding, we gallivanted off to Los Angeles to pursue our career dreams. Just a couple of years later, we welcomed an unplanned but healthy baby boy, who we named James.

Six months later, out of the clear blue and with no medical history to warn me, my life was nearly cut short by a massive stroke caused by an arteriovenous mal-formation (AVM), a congenital brain defect I didn't know I had. I survived by the narrowest of margins and was left with significant, life-altering disabilities. Today, I am unspeakably grateful to be alive, but life is still really, really hard. And it's only getting harder.

In Matthew 5, Jesus said that God blesses those of us who realize our deep need for Him and those of us who have lost what we thought was most important. If these words describe your situation as well as they describe mine, you may be wondering why you don't *feel* all that blessed, even if Jesus says you are.

I asked myself that question more times than I can remember until, one day, I happened upon Isaiah 45:3. "And I will give you treasures hidden in the darkness—secret riches. I will do this so you may know that I am the LORD, the God of Israel, the one who calls you by name" (NLT). The passage is tucked into a much longer series of promises from God to the Israelite people during their exile in Babylon. After decades in the darkness, I can imagine just how beaten-up and broken down these people might have felt. If anyone needed a dose of hope, it was them.

After I read this, it dawned on me: the darkest days of my suffering had taught me things that a pain-free life never could have. In the darkness, I experienced peace that transcended my circumstances. I rediscovered my worth apart from my ability. I gave up the illusion that I was in control of much of anything. None of that could have happened in a life lived exclusively in the light of favorable circumstances.

When I redefined *darkness* as the place in which God's light can shine most brightly, I didn't have to be so afraid of suffering and sorrow anymore. Does this mean that I now run into the darkness with abandon and a shovel, looking to dig up some treasures? No, I'm not completely unhinged! But when I do find myself in the shadows—and I find myself there often—I feel more prepared to learn the right lessons while I'm there.

My pain is too precious to be wasted, so I want to share what I've learned with you. Some of these lessons are for the days when your pain is blinding and your wounds are fresh. Other lessons will be useful when you have a little distance from the epicenter of your suffering. There's a time to hurt and there's a time to heal. And then, I promise you, there will be a time to hope.

If I have to go into the darkness, you'd better believe I'm going to get some treasure out of it. And I know you can too.

TIMELINE

As we explore the treasures to be found in the darkness of our lives, I'll be drawing on memories and experiences from my own life. These anecdotes and musings won't be presented in a linear or chronological order (welcome to my brain—it's a bit wild in here!), so I'm providing you with a handy little timeline that should help you orient yourself to the arc of my good/hard story.

- 1982: I am born in Athens, Georgia.

- 1990s: I spend the summers of my childhood at Camp DeSoto.

- 2000–2004: I attend Samford University in Birmingham, Alabama, where I meet my now husband, Jay.

- FALL 2004: Jay and I are married.

- 2005: We move from the Deep South to Los Angeles, where Jay attends law school and I work in acting and modeling.

- 2007: Our son James is born.

- APRIL 21, 2008: I suffer a massive brain stem stroke at age twenty-six and spend forty days in the ICU.

- AUGUST 2008: I move into a residential neurological rehab facility to relearn to walk, talk, and swallow.

- SUMMER 2012: I fall at my parents' home in Georgia and severely break my leg.

- 2013: My neurologist discovers and operates on an aneurysm in my brain, totally unconnected to my stroke in 2008.

- 2015: Our miracle baby, John, is born.

- MAY 2017: I develop multiple life-threatening vertebral artery dissections.

- JUNE 2017: We host our first sessions of Hope Heals Camp in Alabama.

- SUMMER 2018: We move from Los Angeles to Atlanta.

- FALL 2018: My dad is diagnosed with a rare cancer called multiple myeloma.

- 2019: My medical team confirms that I have an ultrarare and undiagnosable neurovascular disorder.

- 2020: I fall while riding an adaptive bike and severely injure my right leg again.

- 2022: Jay and I celebrate our fortieth birthdays (exactly three weeks apart).

PART ONE

FOR THE HURTING

Losing the Lives We Wanted

1

DISBELIEF

The moment my doctor said the word, a pit opened up in my stomach and threatened to swallow me whole, sanity and all. *Aneurysm.*

Just five years before, I had survived what should have been an unsurvivable brain hemorrhage. These crazy, one-in-a-million neurovascular phenomena were supposed to be behind me. *Been there, done that, hated every second. Thanks for the memories!* But during a routine checkup in 2014, my neurosurgeon identified a new abnormality nestled in a grainy black-and-white scan of my brain: an aneurysm on the "good" side of my brain that had been left unscathed by my stroke. The stroke had already left me with facial paralysis, double vision, total loss of balance and fine motor coordination, and partial deafness. What further damage would this aneurysm wreak if it ruptured?

My doctors determined they would never be able to reliably predict whether or not the aneurysm would rupture, but knowing it was there left me with a dreadful decision. I could take my chances and choose no intervention, or I could elect to have an operation to "coil" the aneurysm and consent to every risk you'd assume comes along with brain surgery. Death included.

After a thousand conversations with Jay, our families, and God, I decided to move forward with the coiling surgery. As the date of the operation approached, I'd never felt so nervous in my entire life. Since my stroke, I'd had more than ten operations, but none since my initial lifesaving surgery had involved my brain. And that first one had been a surprise to me, so I'd been spared any presurgery anxiety.

The night before the operation—a night that could have been my last—a group of people gathered at our church to pray for me. As Jay wheeled me into the room, a dear friend approached and kneeled in front of my wheelchair. She gripped both my hands in hers, held my gaze for a long moment, then offered the most comforting words I had ever heard.

"I cannot believe this is happening to you," she said through a mist of tears. "I just can't believe it."

In that moment, this straight-shooting validation of my pain was more useful to me than any Bible verse or eloquent word of encouragement. My friend recognized the utter ludicrousness of my situation and sat with me in the wide-eyed shock of it all. She accompanied me into the necessary process of lament instead of trying to force me into a place of acceptance. She was asking questions about God's goodness on my behalf instead of reminding me that God was good. In that moment, divine provision looked like a friend who felt just as hurt and confused as I did. And I sure was thankful for the comfort of good company on that hard day.

That awful, unexpected aneurysm taught me there is a time for learning lessons, but first there is a time for complete disbelief. The first step in accepting my circumstances was to allow those circumstances to bewilder my mind and break my heart. And, friend, the same grace is being extended to you. Allow yourself to feel the shock and the sickness and the hurt. I promise you won't stay there, but you've got to start there.

Eventually, I was able to believe what was happening to me. I was even able to believe there might be deep purpose in all this pain. But first, I needed permission *not* to believe it.

If it's true for me, could it be true for you too?

THE FIRST STEP IN HEALING IS ALLOWING MY
STORY TO BREAK MY OWN HEART.

A DEATH REFLECTION

Have you ever given up anything for Lent? I've always really liked the idea of sharing in a season of repentance and reflection with the global Christian community. I mean, in theory. Despite my good intentions, I almost never remember Lent is happening until we're already three or four days in. At that point, I'm deep into the leftover king cake, and I've already spent several hours watching TV and scrolling mindlessly on my phone. So sugar, television, and social media fasts have to be struck from the list, right? Then I scramble to find some treat or habit I haven't indulged in since Lent began. I usually squeak by with something slightly less concrete, like gossiping or complaining. (It still counts! You know you've done it too.)

During a recent Lenten season, a friend posted online about her fascinating decision to give up her "illusion of immortality." Intense, I know. She explained that if Lent prepares us to observe the role of death in Christ's story, it should also prepare us to confront the role of death in our own stories. So for forty days she set aside time to actively acknowledge and reflect on her eventual death and the deaths of all the people she loves. (Needless to say, she's a riot at parties!)

As I followed her online revelations, I had a revelation of my own. By very different means and without consent, I had given up my illusion of immortality too. At twenty-six years old, I'd seen and touched and tasted death. To me, it was no longer an abstraction. It was an actual experience, and now I had to decide what to do with that. I'm most tempted to dig in my heels to denial. To deflect with empty optimism. To numb out to the pain (hence the king cake and the TV and the scrolling). I want to do whatever the *opposite* of a Lenten death reflection is.

At the end of my friend's forty-day practice, she shared how she'd come to understand that death is not something to be denied, avoided, or even begrudgingly accepted. Death makes the expanse of a lifetime finite and therefore precious. Death is like the gilded frame that gives definition to our living days. It's the built-in counterbalance that throws all beauty and goodness and aliveness into greater relief. Death is not to be ignored.

I think all this is true of literal, end-of-life death. But it's also true of all our losses. What is loss if not a type of death, after all? The death of a dream or a relationship or an ability. Before my online friend could see death for what it really was, she had to be brave enough to get on eye level with it, spend time with it, and call it by its name. The same, I think, can be said for our losses.

Ignoring loss, denying grief, numbing out to pain, or strong-arming our souls into premature closure are all such tempting tactics. But these routes are less than useful. And maybe even harmful in the long run. Before we can heal, we have to grieve what's been lost. We have to look at our empty hands and feel the heavy absence of the thing we loved. Naming our hurts is the beginning of seeing the goodness of our lives with clearer eyes. What is grief, after all, if not leftover love? To mourn a loss is to recognize a good gift you had.

To take its full form, resurrection requires both life and loss. I learned that from Jesus Himself, who died a very real death to prove that a second-chance life is available to us, both literally and in the intangible areas of life. When I don't name the deaths and the losses and the hurts, I rob myself of the full experience of the new life that follows. If death is inevitable, it might as well be useful.

If it's true for me, could it be true for you too?

BEFORE I CAN HEAL, I HAVE TO GRIEVE WHAT'S BEEN LOST.

3

SPRINTING TOWARD SUFFERING

Sometimes I can't believe how this all started. Back when I was twenty-six, before anyone had any idea something was brewing in my brain stem, I'd been busy cooking a lasagna to deliver to some new friends in the community we were building in LA. Jay had made an unusual midday stop by our apartment to print out a final law school paper and arrived just in time to find me slumped face-first on the kitchen floor, vomiting violently. He immediately called 911. Soon a crush of emergency responders flooded our little home and loaded me into an ambulance. Jay gathered our sleeping baby into our hand-me-down SUV and followed the ambulance that was whisking me down the Pacific Coast Highway and into a future full of unknowns.

In my last moments of lucidity, I told Jay to call our friend Anna to take care of James. Even in what should have been my dying breaths, I was managing logistics. Classic Katherine.

Jay barreled down the highway and arranged for Anna to meet him at the hospital. As Jay skidded into the hospital parking lot, he saw movement in his side-view mirror. There was Anna, who was visibly pregnant with her first baby, sprinting toward his car. Sprinting toward his suffering.

While I was not present for this moment and would remain largely unconscious for the next few months, Anna's arrival on the scene of our waking nightmare remains one of the most potent reflections of Jesus I've ever heard of. On the worst days of our lives, no intervention—short of a miracle—could be more heartening and healing than a beloved friend running toward the darkness of our pain.

Jay could have ignored my instructions. He sure had done it before! He could have kept the pain private to prevent appearing overly dramatic or like he was asking too much from our friends. Instead, he embraced Anna with open arms and admitted, "We need you. We need you. We need you."

Every human instinct within us recoils from exposing our pain. Inviting other people into the ugly, unresolved mess of our suffering is humiliating. And it comes at the steep price of vulnerability.

What pain are you clutching close to your chest today? What suffering needs to be shared?

Jesus often rerouted His journey to intentionally intersect with suffering people. That's what His trip to earth was all about. The Gospels tell how people were healed because Jesus engaged their pain, yes. But they were also healed because they *allowed* Him to engage their pain.

Isolation is often the deepest wound inflicted by suffering of all kinds. But when the diagnosis proves chronic or the windfall never arrives or the would-be nursery sits empty, we are not sentenced to bearing the burden alone. When God sends someone sprinting toward your pain, you better open your arms wide to receive them. There is no bravery in doing the hard stuff alone. We can bear our suffering when we are willing to share our suffering.

Anna would go on to care for baby James for months as Jay and I navigated the journey back from the edge of death. She was a fixture in the hospital waiting room, often toting James in one arm and bags of food in the other. I've been healed by the showing-up and staying-put of Anna and a dozen other saints. All because we invited them into the suffering, and they accepted without hesitation.

If it's true for me, could it be true for you too?

I CAN BEAR MY SUFFERING WHEN I AM
WILLING TO SHARE MY SUFFERING.

4

IN THE DARK

In 2017 I stared up at the ceiling, a sad beige grid of speckled acoustic tiles. Deep into my third consecutive day lying in a hospital bed with my neck cradled in a thick brace, I couldn't ignore the grip of panic tightening around my mind any longer. Being in a hospital wasn't making me panic. But being *awake* in a hospital sure was.

After the stroke that had changed my life in 2008, I lay in an ICU bed for a full forty days in a state of semiconsciousness. I have almost no memory of that time. From there I was moved to an acute rehabilitation unit, where my days were filled with therapy and visitors. Even then, my mind was foggy at best. I wasn't fully aware of what was happening around me or to me, and I certainly wasn't doing a lot of introspection. I would go on to have thirteen major operations, which meant I frequented many hospitals, but I rarely stayed in each one more than a night. I was almost always under a thick haze of anesthetics and medication.

One morning in the summer of 2017, after days of some mild dizziness and neck pain I'd tried my best to ignore, I had a fainting spell that led to the discovery of multiple life-threatening vertebral artery dissections. That landed me in the hospital for five long days. Five unmedicated, wide-awake, painfully clearheaded days replete with enough time to ruminate and worry and go a tiny bit crazy.

Severe double vision doesn't allow for much enjoyable reading, phone scrolling, or TV watching, so I exhausted my entertainment options almost immediately. I was left to face my own thoughts, which was a rare occurrence for me. As a mom, nonprofit founder, and professional speaker, my poststroke life had never had much silence or stillness. I felt deeply uncomfortable with the sudden excess of both.

Instinctively, I shied away from the bottomless pit of questions and unresolved trauma stored inside my mind. Isn't it always easier to distract, after all? I was faced with a few options: I could avoid the pain, I could lose myself in the fear, or I could choose to activate the hope that I had written and spoken about for so long.

Spoiler alert: I chose hope.

With nothing but time stretching out before me, I began the invisible and intense work of telling my own story to myself. With my soul as the singular member of the audience, I preached the well-worn, hard-won truths of the past decade of my life like a liturgy. These words were no longer talking points. They were a lifeline.

When you find yourself in pitch-black suffering again, what truths will help you find your bearings in the darkness? Now is the time to identify them. To hold them. To press them into your soul. Here, take mine, if you need a place to start:

> Suffering is not the end of my story. Pain and joy can coexist. New life always begins with the end of an old life. My hope is not in any good gift but in the Giver of every good gift. God made me to do the hard things in the good story He is writing for my life.

These lessons learned—and the hundred more I spoke over myself that day— won't magically take away the sadness or fear. But they sure can help us face the sadness and fear with a little more hope. During those five wide-awake days in that hospital bed, I proved to myself that the lessons of the past were still true in the present. And I think it's safe to say they'll be true in the future too. My future and yours.

Now I can say for certain that what is true in the light is still true in the dark.

If it's true for me, could it be true for you too?

WHAT IS TRUE IN THE LIGHT IS STILL TRUE IN THE DARK.

5

THE PAGE WILL TURN

S hould I have died?

I asked myself this question one evening as Jay connected a plastic hose to the gastrostomy tube, or G-tube, port in my abdomen. Three times a day, he fed a thick liquid through a tube in my stomach. I hadn't eaten a bite of food in the six months since my stroke, and nothing made me question my survival more than the mental and physical hunger that gnawed away at me day and night. I couldn't eat or walk or take care of my son. I was suspended between life and death, and neither side seemed to want me. I hung in that hellish in-between for a full year.

As I look back on this relatively short but horribly painful time in my life, I can see it as the first chapter in a really good story. But at the time, it looked like the ending to me. The possibilities of my second-chance life had been completely swallowed up by grief for my first life, and there was no relief in sight. The reality is I was stuck. In between. I couldn't fast-forward to the good part. I just had to go through it.

I can't go back and have a conversation with the Katherine of the past, the Katherine who was being fed through a G-tube and was barely able to sit upright on her own. But I can speak to you. Maybe you're suspended between your own versions of life and death right now. I need you to know that your story doesn't end there.

Maybe you've decided you simply cannot handle your life any longer. Maybe you're carrying emotional trauma you should never have to bear, or gritting your teeth through physical pain that is certifiably impossible to stand. Every last one of us lives on some point of the suffering spectrum. And if your pain feels insignificant at the moment, one day it won't feel that way. We all will be overwhelmed by suffering if we live long enough. If things don't seem so bad today, hang on to my words for when they do.

When the pain feels too big, hold on. Stay tuned. Our lives are stories that God is writing, and the plot is always moving forward. Your story is made up of chapters, many of which will be great and others that will be forgettable. And some chapters will be terrible beyond words, but that doesn't mean the big story can't be beautiful and deeply good.

Because our lives are stories, we don't have to put so much pressure on this moment. The moment may hurt so, so badly. But soon the moment will pass and the page will turn. You'll look back and understand that God made you to do hard things in the good story He is writing for your life. And once you've endured the suffering once, you will know you can do it again.

These days I understand that if I should have died, I would have died. My story wasn't over. In fact, the best chapters were still ahead of me, although I never could have believed it in the early days of my recovery. I can honestly say that the story I never would have chosen is the story I don't think I would choose to change.

If it's true for me, could it be true for you too?

GOD MADE ME TO DO HARD THINGS IN THE
GOOD STORY HE IS WRITING FOR MY LIFE.

6

THE KNOT

"Who is that? Where did he come from?"

"*Shhh*, I don't know. I've never seen this movie before."

"Wait, what did she just say? Why is she wearing that big hat? Could you rewind it?"

"*Mooooom!*"

This recurring Friday night exchange is why my sons keep threatening to ban me from Wolf family movie time. Replace the exasperated *"Mom!"* with *"Katherine!"* and you'll see why Jay swore off watching movies with me when we were dating. According to my own mother, I came out of the womb with a question on my lips and haven't stopped asking them since.

Asking questions is how I make sense of the world around me. I won't apologize for it! To me, questions offer chances for vulnerability, invitations into humility, and opportunities to see that our doubts don't make God turn away from us. What a beautiful thing!

But because I love questions, I also really love answers. For a while, I was pretty convinced I could find any answer if I asked the right questions of the right people. Mystery was a barrier to knowing God and it only cropped up, I believed, when I asked the wrong questions. When any unknowable-ness persisted in my life, I stifled it. The world was supposed to make sense, simple as that. There was an answer for every question.

Well, the world stopped making sense when I almost died, without warning, from a massive stroke. That's when the real questions began. I wouldn't be able to speak out loud for months after my stroke, but with the electronic letter board I was given, I'd slowly punch out the questions that were racing around my mind on an endless loop. That loop eventually formed a theological knot of suffering between my heart and my head that I would fumble to untie for years. *Why did this happen to me? How will I go on? What is the purpose of all this pain? Does God exist, and could He really be good?*

If you're holding this book in your hands, you must have some questions. Dear one, please hear me when I tell you that your questions are not offensive to God, and they certainly aren't a barrier to intimacy with Him. They are not from the Enemy. They don't come from a lack of faith. Your questions are actually the unmissable first step toward healing. Your questions prove that you have not given up. Your questions are evidence of a hope that, somewhere out there, reason and goodness and order exist. As if you're extending a hand to your heavenly Father and saying, "Let me know You more," your questions connect you to God Himself.

More than fifteen years later, I'm still asking some of the very same questions I asked from my hospital bed. Many have been answered, by time or wise friends or Scripture. But just as many remain unresolved. My pain continues to beg questions I can't answer, but I'm realizing that answers might not be the end goal after all. What if the theological knot of suffering isn't asking to be untied? What if the very act of grappling with the knot is tethering us to a God who has all the answers, even when we don't?

I'm still asking questions out loud—in prayer, in community, and yes, during movie night. Acknowledging these overwhelming unknowns in the presence of God and alongside other hurting people has healed the shame and isolation wreaked by holding my doubts alone. Allowing questions to go unanswered remains one of the great challenges of my life, but the risk is worth the intimacy to be found in the very act of asking.

If it's true for me, could it be true for you too?

MY QUESTIONS AREN'T OFFENSIVE TO GOD.
IN FACT, THEY CONNECT ME TO HIM.

7

THE GOOD LIFE

H as anyone you know learned to swallow again after over a year without eating?" I asked. My words still sounded thick and unwieldy in my mouth in those first months of relearning to talk.

The woman across the table from me fiddled with her equipment. "Let's try that applesauce again, hmm?"

She wasn't getting off the hook that easily. Undeterred, I tried again.

"Am I ever going to eat?"

No answer.

My speech therapist rose from her seat to adjust one of the dozen electrodes stuck to my neck. "Okay, I want you to press your tongue to the roof of your mouth now."

Seriously?! The nerve of this lady! I pondered trying to nip at her finger as she brought an ice chip to my lips for the next exercise. She and I had performed variations on this little song and dance several times a week during our year of swallowing therapy. I hadn't eaten food since my stroke and my hunger had developed into a kind of chronic pain, which I channeled into a single-minded search for even one story about a patient successfully eating again after going as long as I had without a swallowing reflex.

In hindsight, I understand my therapist was kind enough to know that giving me false hope could be more harmful than giving me no hope at all. Hope was all I was really looking for, after all, not a story of someone who had learned to swallow again. I was grasping for the possibility that a good life—a life worth living—was waiting on the other side of this catastrophe. And isn't that the question at the bottom of every experience with pain? *Will life ever be good again?*

Before my stroke, I really loved Psalm 84:11, a verse that tells us God "withholds no good thing from those who walk with integrity" (NASB). That verse became more confusing than inspiring the day I lost most of my physical capabilities, my ability to do motherhood the way I wanted, and my career. God was not merely withholding a good life from me, it seemed; He was taking my good life away from me. I would wrestle with this tension for years, both for myself and for everyone else living lives the world would call anything but "good."

Then my definition of *good* was turned upside down when I read the words of sixteenth-century theologian Sir Richard Baker. "The good things of God," he wrote, "are chiefly Peace of conscience, and joy in the Holy Ghost, in this life; Fruition of God's Presence, and Vision of his blessed Face, in the next."[1] Because I can't resist alliteration, I've come up with a snappy way to remember Baker's meaning: "The truly good things in life are God's peace, presence, and provision in the process."

When I dared to measure my circumstances with a new rubric, I found that there was a good life on the other side of my suffering. I'm living it! In fact, I can see the truly good things—God's peace, presence, and provision—more plainly now that all the noise of my independence, ability, and self-determination has been cleared away. Would it be possible for you to believe that some of what you lost was static, that it was stifling the truly good stuff?

For me, this reframing of goodness is not natural, even to this day. But when I'm sitting in a season of suffering and asking, *Will life ever be good again?* I can believe it will be. I can survey my situation and see how God is giving me peace that transcends my circumstances. How He is sticking with me in the thick of my sadness. Who He is providing to help me along the way. A good life was waiting for me when I was willing to redefine what goodness really was.

If it's true for me, could it be true for you too?

WHEN I REDEFINE WHAT GOODNESS MEANS, I CAN
FIND GOODNESS IN THE MIDST OF MY SUFFERING.

8

THE GIFTS OR THE GIVER

My parents and two little sisters stood at the finish line of the high school cross country meet. Every other runner had completed the course except me, and my family was not entirely surprised that I'd be finishing decidedly and completely last. They waited and waited, wondering if I had somehow found an ice cream truck along the path or struck up a conversation with a friendly squirrel.

Turns out, I had fainted. With the entire pack of my fellow runners a solid quarter mile ahead of me, I had started to feel dizzy. After losing consciousness midstride and rolling down a gently sloping embankment, I eventually came to, covered in grass stains but otherwise unscathed. I got to my feet and slowly meandered to the end of the course, where my family cheered me over the finish line as if I were in the running for an Olympic medal.

This classic Katherine mishap became a favorite tale in our family lore. It would take years to understand that stories like this—of clumsiness and dizziness and stunning feats of unathleticism—were actually warning signs of the brain malformation that eventually caused my stroke. And on top of that, my stroke was only the first in a series of near-lethal brain events that have tried to take me out altogether over the last decade and a half.

Recently, my doctors labeled my situation as an "undiagnosable neurovascular disorder." Real helpful, right? While that description doesn't provide many details, it tells me all I really need to know: there is suffering ahead for me. And I am still coming to terms with that.

But if I'm being honest, if the aneurysms or vertebral dissections don't kill me, sometimes I think the heartbreak inherent in being a human might do the job.

Disability has been hard, yes. Trauma has been hard, of course. But so has my marriage. And my family of origin. And my insecurities. And parenting. And a thousand other wounds that exist completely separate from my stroke. Surviving one near-death experience doesn't exempt me from experiencing pain in all kinds of different ways. Your pain may be one-in-a-million or run-of-the-mill, but to be human is to be hurting. So it's natural to ask, *What can we get out of all this pain?*

Turns out, we can get God Himself. If I ever believed God played by a rule book or that reality could be easily understood, receiving this neurovascular diagnosis (or nondiagnosis, really) relieved me of that illusion. Suffering has affirmed that God is God, and I am not. It has taken me by the hand, guided me to a crossroads, and asked, "What is it you want from God? Do you want the gifts, or do you want the Giver Himself?"

Maybe you're standing in that place today, realizing you've been grasping for the life you thought you deserved, the gifts you thought you were entitled to. All along, the Giver of every good and perfect gift has been there, offering Himself to you. To receive God, however, means meeting Him on His terms. It means unraveling every definition of goodness and every expectation we have for our lives. In the undoing, we can come to know a God who is more mysterious and merciful than we ever imagined. And we can become versions of ourselves who are more openhanded and unencumbered than we've ever been.

Which gifts are keeping you from receiving more of the Giver? While I may never be able to open my hands all the way, I'm opening up space for God to tell me who He really is. He is still introducing Himself to me, but the God I am getting to know is more magnificent and mystifying than the gifts I thought I wanted.

If it's true for me, could it be true for you too?

SUFFERING CONFRONTS ME WITH THE QUESTION, *WHAT IS IT I WANT FROM GOD? DO I WANT THE GIFTS, OR DO I WANT THE GIVER HIMSELF?*

9

HOPE WHILE YOU COPE

I don't like surprises. What I do like is a plan. I boast a mystifying ability to store plans, schedules, and logistics in my mind. Can I wing it? Sure! Would I rather work out every contingency in minute and excruciating detail? Absolutely. I am easily frustrated by the human plight of being confined to time and space. I want to know how we will get from point A to point B. And, while I'm at it, I might as well figure out how we're getting to point Z as well.

Befriending our now-ness can free us from the temptation to fill today with the worries of tomorrow. But what do we do when the here and now hurts?

If your brain is like mine, it has a stubborn (but understandable) tendency to get stuck when it's experiencing pain, emptiness, and despair. We can't just fast-forward to see our happy endings, which leaves us with a gap between reality and resolution.

Before He died, Jesus told His friends that He'd be back and that death wouldn't have the final word. But when He was crucified, they still abandoned all hope. And who can blame them? I think you and I will probably spend most of our lives feeling like Jesus' friends on the day of His death—disappointed and desperate, stuck in the thick of pre-resurrection darkness. But just like Jesus' friends, we've also been told that all our stories, and the world's big story, will end in redemption. After all, the Christ story extends beyond a single time or place. It's the totally universal yet deeply personal story of against-all-odds hope.

Relying on God's promise to make all things new will probably never become reflexive for you or me. So we've got to resolve to live as resurrection people, people who know in their bones that there is life beyond our crosses and hope beyond the "Good Fridays" of life. When we can't tap into second-chance hope from our own experiences, we are invited to borrow the hope of Jesus' second-chance life.

No, we're not Jesus. And yes, we are human, and we can't do much to change that. No matter how deeply we know and love the gospel story, true joy and peace can feel inaccessible on our darkest days. Because we can't reach into the future to see how this all ends. But we can choose to practice resurrection hope. Like a discipline, we can use that borrowed hope on the good days, the hard days, and the ordinary days. Hope while you cope, I call it. And it's a whole lot of work. But does it pay off? You know it does.

Despite the best and most detailed plans I can make, both the pain and beauty of my life continue to surprise me and always will. While the specifics of my story's ending remain a mystery for now, the character of God does not. I can plan on His resurrection power being present with me now and meeting me at the end. And that gives me so much hope for today and tomorrow.

If it's true for me, could it be true for you too?

WHEN I CAN'T FIND HOPE IN MY OWN EXPERIENCES, I CAN BORROW THE HOPE OF JESUS' SECOND-CHANCE LIFE.

10

FOUNDATIONS 101

The storms of life are coming for everyone. You better build your life and your identity on the rock-solid foundation of faith in Jesus, rather than the shifting sands of your expectations of yourself, each other, or the world."

My almost-father-in-law's bright voice resounded through the sanctuary and snapped my wandering attention back into the moment. I was standing at the altar of my own wedding ceremony, my hands interlocked with Jay's. A seasoned pastor, Jay's father stood before us as he officiated the service. My mind had drifted away into the surreal dreaminess of the moment, but hearing the word *storms* jerked me into the present. In my nine months of wedding planning, it hadn't occurred to me to review the notes for the ceremony sermon. I'd just assumed he'd play the hits, like the love chapter or something!

Although I didn't expect to hear it at my own wedding, the message tucked into our marriage sermon was a message I'd heard, by God's grace, my entire life: our foundation matters. No amount of preparation can prevent life's storms, but a strong foundation—being grounded in the ultimate truth of who we are and what matters most—can help us weather the storms well.

As I stood at that altar and exchanged vows with Jay, I never could have predicted the storm that was already brewing under my gauzy wedding veil. Buried deep in my brain, a malformed tangle of blood vessels was waiting to burst.

Our ceremony spilled into a midday reception full of dancing and deep-fried Southern delicacies. The party would continue for the first few years of our marriage. Each day seemed a bright new opportunity for adventure and delight. Even so, my father-in-law's words—which were really the words of Jesus—remained planted deep in our hearts. Together, Jay and I built our foundation with intention . . . or as much intention as a pair of slightly flighty twenty-two-year-olds can pull off. Luckily for us, Jesus provided pretty great assembly instructions for building a strong foundation in Matthew 7.

For us, building a foundation looked like praying with persistence (v. 7). It looked like investing our time and energy into a local church community and developing empathy for the people around us (v. 12). It meant practicing generous forgiveness and refusing to major on minor offenses (vv. 1–5). And most of all, it meant believing that God was deeply good and that we were fully loved by Him (v. 11).

A few years after our wedding day, the storm that came in the form of a brain stem stroke blew away every last bit of the life Jay and I had built together. (We're talking Dorothy in the center of the tornado here, people. And we certainly did not look as cute as a wide-eyed, pigtailed Judy Garland.) But because we'd invested some real sweat equity into developing a rock-solid hope in Jesus to make all things new and forming bone-deep identities as children of a good God, our foundation survived the storm when almost nothing else did.

What parts of your life could withstand a category 5 hurricane? At the core of your soul, there is an indestructible *something*, an unyielding reality that you are loved, seen, and provided for by God. If you're willing to build your foundation well—and with a thick layer of God's grace—it can resist the crush of any kind of suffering. In fact, a storm won't blow you off a foundation like this; rather, a storm can press you deeper into the safety of your foundation.

Even after all the pain and disappointments I've faced, I'm still tempted to build my life on the shifting sands of my own desires or the expectations I have of the world. Who isn't, after all? But, darn it, it's never long before another storm comes, and I'm reminded to continue following Jesus' assembly instructions. I'll keep nurturing that indestructible identity that says God is my Father, and I belong to Him.

Piece by piece, I'll keep building my life on the Rock of Ages. When the storms of life come—and, boy, will they come!—I'll be as ready as I can be. And one day, to borrow the words often attributed to Charles Spurgeon, I may even "learn to kiss the waves that throw me up against the Rock of Ages."[2]

If it's true for me, could it be true for you too?

I CAN BUILD A FOUNDATION OF TRUST IN GOD'S PLAN
AND AN INDESTRUCTIBLE IDENTITY AS HIS BELOVED,
WHICH CAN RESIST THE CRUSH OF SUFFERING.

11

MORE

At the beginning of 2008, our church small group decided we each would select a word for the year and share them with one another at our first gathering of the year. Jay and I chose our words with great care and spiritual import—on the drive to our small group gathering. What can I say? We tend to procrastinate.

My chosen word was the audacious *more*. Even after a whirlwind season of getting married, moving across the country, pursuing work in the entertainment industry, and giving birth to a baby boy, I knew deep down that there was even *more* waiting for me. Jay was dubious and hoped that the coming year would be a "less is more" situation. His word was probably something more practical, like *clarity* or *patience*.

That quiet inkling within me wasn't a hunger for more stuff or career advancement. I can only describe it as a persistent longing for a new depth of experience and formation of character. I guess I wanted more of God, even though I had no clue what that actually meant.

Less than four months after that optimistic request for *more*, I would be lying in an intensive care unit, all but dead.

I spent the first months after my stroke in a comalike state, but when the fog slowly lifted, I began grappling with how my year of *more* had turned into a year of utter loss. Loss of autonomy, ability, health, certainty, security, and aspirations. I'd ended up with less, it seemed.

As I surveyed the wreckage, I could have believed that all this loss meant my life had been emptied of any goodness. Turned over and drained dry. But after a careful, slow-motion search, I found *so much more* goodness buried in the rubble than I could have imagined. The stroke laid bare any cheap illusions of goodness in my life so I could see the things that were worth wanting *more* of.

In those early years of my second-chance life, I had the privilege of understanding peace of the soul separate from peace of circumstances. I developed hope in the middle of a really hard story without needing to know the ending. I knew what the presence of God felt like even when absolutely nothing was perfect.

If we allow it, loss leaves space for God to replace our knockoff versions of goodness with His true goodness. For me, that has looked like being grateful for what remained after losing so much. It's meant fully embracing the beauty and brokenness of my life, rather than denying that the two can coexist. And it's meant releasing my grip on what I've felt entitled to in order to receive *more* than I ever deserved.

If it's true for me, could it be true for you too?

LOSS LEAVES SPACE FOR GOD TO REPLACE MY KNOCKOFF
VERSION OF GOODNESS WITH HIS TRUE GOODNESS.

12

THE BLANK PAGE

For as long as I can remember, I've tackled life with an unflappable (some pronounce it "delusional") optimism. I've been called Pollyanna more than once, and I refuse to receive it as an insult because those bows she wore were very chic. Despite my sunny outlook, even I have sunk to places of real hopelessness once or twice in the years since my stroke. These dark spaces were not necessarily full of fear or pain. They just felt altogether absent of the comfort or peace of God's presence. The silence felt unending. My story was unresolved and my pain unredeemed.

Even in the places of hopelessness, I was pacing the well-worn neural pathways of memorizing and meditating on passages from the Bible, as I'd done since I was a child. I had been a dedicated student and lover of Scripture for decades, but these poststroke stretches of desperation brought new meaning to the stories I knew so well.

One of the portions of the Bible that became most important to me, strangely, didn't contain a single written word. The blank page in my Bible that divided the Old Testament from the New Testament suddenly drew my attention as if it were outlined in neon lights. No longer just a tissue-thin page, it became a symbol for the state of my soul.

For *four hundred* long, tumultuous years—after the events in Malachi and before the story picks back up in the book of Matthew—God's people waited in the heavy absence of prophetic words or divine appearances, as far as we know. This situation sounded all too familiar. God knows it felt like four hundred years as I waded through my own disappointment and desperation. In my story and in the Israelites' story, faith became stale, promises rang empty, hope turned to shame, and suffering seemed to bring no redemption at all.

But eventually, the blank page turned. Jesus arrived on the scene in His quiet way and renamed the Israelites' suffering (and the suffering of all of humanity, really) as an opportunity for restoration. He proved the hurt and the silence and waiting were not wasted. Rather, they were the raw materials for resurrection.

In His own time, Jesus arrived in my silent space of suffering too. He didn't airlift me out of my circumstances or miraculously reverse any of the damage to my body. Instead, He began building His kingdom squarely within my hopelessness. And, let me tell you, it was worth the wait.

You may be in your own intertestamental period, a blank page you could mistake as empty of God's presence or purpose. The waiting can feel a whole lot like suffering. But, friend, from experience I know this to be true: Jesus shows up in the silence. He builds His kingdom at the wit's end of our waiting. He repurposes our pain as the building blocks of redemption.

As I live inside the blank pages of my life—and there have been many—the waiting has become oddly sacred. Now I can fill the silence with anticipation rather than dread. And you can too. Hardship by hardship, grace by grace, resurrection by resurrection, He's building me. And He's building His kingdom *through* me. Even when it feels like hundreds of years of silence. Even when I can't see how it will work out. There is a new testament coming.

If it's true for me, could it be true for you too?

JESUS WILL SHOW UP IN THE SILENCE AND BUILD HIS KINGDOM AT THE WIT'S END OF MY WAITING. HE CAN REPURPOSE MY PAIN AS BUILDING BLOCKS OF REDEMPTION.

13

REDEFINING DEATH

If you've known death yourself, I don't have to explain to you that it's far from poetic. It's heinous and messy.

Before I had my brush with death firsthand, I'd never given much thought to the rather central part death plays in the Christian faith. Like, come on, people. It's kinda weird! We can say it out loud. We are people of hope and abundant life who rally around the gruesome, bloody death of an innocent man. We wear crosses around our necks, and many of us even act out our own burials during baptism. We eat the bread and drink the wine to remember a body that had the life beaten out of it.

This eerie, intimate connection to death is woven throughout our faith narrative, and most of us have become immune to the gritty reality it represents. We're really good at appreciating death as an esoteric symbol or the precursor to the rising action of the Easter story. But most of us resist death once it intersects with our flesh-and-blood reality. We'll do anything to avoid it, and rightfully so. It's terrible. I know from experience. And you, dear one, might too.

As the effects of my stroke gradually became evident in the initial months of my recovery, my family and I buried our dreams, identities, and sense of security in an agonizing, slow-motion funeral. Although I did not actually die, many parts of me did. Each of those early poststroke days and weeks presented a fresh chance to discover something else I'd never get back or someone I would never get to be. Even now, a decade and a half later, I'm still realizing things I'll never do. The tomb of my former life continues to be filled to this day.

I bet you have a grave of your own, symbolic or otherwise, that has swallowed up what you love most. Stolen the parts of life you hold closest. Maybe you've buried any hope for redemption alongside your dreams for the future.

As I've navigated my version of the valley of the shadow of death, I've found that true hope is nourished, against all reasoning, in the dark places. My old definition of *hope* only functioned in the context of white-knuckled control over my circumstances. But when I allowed that definition to die, a newer, truer version of hope rose in its place. The grave of loss in my life birthed a steadfast hope that doesn't depend on favorable short-term outcomes. Now my hope is in the final, end-all-be-all redemption at the end of all our suffering. My hope is in a Divine Love that is working behind the scenes to make sense out of all the senselessness, to bring life from the death all around us.

Walking through these shadowy places has loosened my grip on the life I expected to have and opened me up to the resurrected life I have been given. The second-chance life. Jesus' death and resurrection tell the story that's available to all of us. I'm taking my place in the story. And as I encounter death, I also encounter a new life that begins where the old life ended.

If it's true for me, could it be true for you too?

LOSS CAN BIRTH A STEADFAST HOPE THAT DOESN'T
DEPEND ON FAVORABLE SHORT-TERM OUTCOMES.

14

HUNGRY

Just before Thanksgiving 2008, six months after I survived my stroke, it hit me: I wouldn't be able to eat Thanksgiving dinner. For a lady as hungry as I was, this particular blow was a total knockout. I had yet to regain my ability to eat food, or even swallow an ice chip, safely.

Most of us would miss food terribly after half a year without eating it. But to understand the depth of my grief here, you should know I am a foodie, through and through. And not just a *Chef's Table*, artisan coffee, foie gras foodie. I've never met a food I didn't like. Give me those soft, weirdly pale grocery store cookies with an inch of pastel icing and the charred baseball-game hot dog with relish from a packet and that squishy, green Jell-O "salad" that only qualifies as a salad in the South. I'll take it all.

So in the weeks leading up to Thanksgiving, this foodie had become all but obsessed with the idea of partaking in an enormous holiday meal. Specifically, an enormous, glistening turkey leg. (Hilarious, I know. Chronic hunger will humble you.)

At that point, I had already failed eight swallowing tests. But I just *knew* God was going to miraculously heal the necessary neurons in my beat-up brain just in time to give me a seat at the feast. I had grand plans to praise Him from dawn till dusk on Thanksgiving Day with my huge turkey leg in hand. What a day it would be, and God would get all the glory!

Instead, on Thanksgiving week I failed the swallowing test a ninth time. My family, unsure of how to handle such a strange and tender day, took shifts eating Thanksgiving lunch out of sight in the kitchen while I sat in my recliner in the living room. No seat at the table, no turkey leg in hand. Not even able to wrangle my newly walking baby or pitch in with the dishes.

Have You forgotten about me, God? I wondered. *Would I be better off dead? At least then I wouldn't be so hungry.*

My hunger was physical, but at the deepest level, it was also spiritual. I was hungry for answers, for resolution, for my life to make sense again. If you're enduring a famine of the soul today, you are as ravenously hungry as I was. While I obsessed over a turkey leg (like a bona fide weirdo), your hopes are fixed on something too. A restored relationship. Long-awaited parenthood. Recovery that finally sticks.

Dear one, let me affirm to you that hungering for something good is not wrong. But in this broken world, bad things can keep us from getting the goodness we crave. You are not being punished or tested. You are passing through a dry land full of wants en route to a perfect place free of need. I pray so many of your hunger pangs are relieved this side of heaven. But even more, I pray you and I can persevere through seasons of emptiness, sustained by a hope that this journey ends in total fulfillment.

So much of what I've lost has yet to be restored, and probably never will be. And the same might be true for you. But I believe one day I'll sit at the heavenly feast of my wildest dreams. Perhaps there will even be platters of turkey legs as far as the eye can see! I won't have to wait for any more miracles because every hope will be fulfilled. And I won't even have to hope anymore, because I'll be face-to-face with Jesus, my hope personified.

If it's true for me, could it be true for you too?

I CAN PERSEVERE THROUGH SEASONS OF EMPTINESS, SUSTAINED BY A HOPE THAT THE JOURNEY ENDS IN TOTAL FULFILLMENT.

15

MEETING MYSELF

My first baby, James, had just turned a year old, and his warm golden hair was long enough to curl up at the tips. He could toddle everywhere by himself. And I couldn't toddle anywhere by myself. (Yeah, finding yourself jealous of a toddler is a certifiable low point.)

What good am I now? I thought as I watched Jay chase our baby around the room. *I can't even pick up my own son.* It was true. I couldn't do much at that point, but I could throw one rager of a pity party.

The moment I lost most of my physical abilities was the moment I met myself, truly, for the first time. As a firstborn, type A achiever, my greatest nightmare had been realized. I was "useless" by all accounts. Without the props of typical independence, achievement, or productivity, I was left to find out what Katherine Wolf was actually worth to the world, to myself, and to God.

I convinced myself that I was virtually worthless, mostly because I was unable to tackle most of my to-do list as a mother and a wife. But on one of the most hopeless days of my early recovery, out of nowhere, God communicated His estimation of my value to me. He laid to rest the lies I was telling—and believing!—about my uselessness. Like a voice memo straight from His heart to my head, He whispered, *Katherine, I don't make mistakes. I have chosen you for this life and I know what I am doing. You are worthy of the special calling you have received. Now go live like it.*

Years after that dispatch of divine insight, God continues to blow up every expectation and disappointment that once overpowered my hope for a good future after my stroke. He helped me see that He is using the very thing that disabled my body to enable His message of unconditional belovedness and belonging to reach countless people. And to reach my own heart while He's at it. He introduced me to myself. And as it turns out, she's really, really loved.

In retrospect, I can laugh (and cringe) at the idea that my value could be earned. *Great job making that bed, Katherine. God definitely loves you a little more after seeing those crisp corners and that karate-chopped throw pillow!* Like, what was I thinking? But as ridiculous as it sounds, you're probably doing some version of the same bad math. Be honest. What do you believe is earning you a place in God's family today?

The overachiever in me is as present as ever, but her intensity has been tempered by the bittersweet reality of my limitations. While my stroke caused some of my outward limitations, it merely exposed the inward limitations that had always been there. There was a time when I resented and resisted them. But now they relentlessly remind me that I am cherished by God just as I am. No qualifiers or conditions. I am loved, and so are you. Full stop.

Maybe, like me, you've been forced into a slower pace—whether by sickness or grief or unfulfilled longings—and that's left you feeling useless in a world obsessed with measurable value. Maybe you could use a reminder of the reality of who you are, which is all too often obscured by the expectations of who you think you should be and what you should offer.

After years of convincing from God Himself, I learned the true source of my value, which happens to be the source of your value too: God's divine decision to give us life and His never-ending commitment to call us beloved. No matter what we do—or don't—accomplish. Today I believe I am worthy of belovedness and belonging, but I couldn't earn them if I tried.

If it's true for me, could it be true for you too?

I AM WORTHY OF BELOVEDNESS AND BELONGING—
AND I COULDN'T EARN THEM IF I TRIED.

16

HANDLE WITH CARE

Here's a pro tip for any typically abled people who may be reading this: just because a person uses a wheelchair does not necessarily mean they cannot understand you when you speak to them. The part of the brain that controls mobility doesn't have much to do with the ears. Wild, I know!

Almost daily, well-intentioned strangers interact with me by nearly yelling their words, using comically large hand gestures, speaking very slowly, or—worst of all—just directing the conversation at Jay, even when it pertains to me. Sometimes people who clearly speak English greet me in a language other than English, a kind of baby talk. I still can't make sense of that one!

These situations can be frustrating and humiliating, but I've identified a pretty powerful truth buried in the ickiness. My *outside* communicates to everyone around me that I am not well *inside*. This could stir up shame or embarrassment in me, sure. But instead, the lack of pretense actually makes me feel immensely fortunate. Because you know what? I am *not* well! Yes, I have a lot of physical issues going on, but my mind and soul are actually just as fragile and busted-up as my body is. People see my outer disabilities and treat me with a little extra care, which means they are treating my *insides* with extra care too. Even if the care is a tad misguided sometimes, I'm still grateful to receive it.

For a long time, I've wanted to produce a T-shirt with bold letters across the front that read "FRAGILE: PLEASE HANDLE WITH CARE" because I recognize that every last one of us is hurting in some way. While Jay has tactfully shut down my big plans for a T-shirt empire, the sentiment remains. Whether you have visible dis-abilities or not, you have invisible pain that deserves tender handling by the people around you. Whatever your pain may be today—grief, disappointment, loneliness, abandonment—I want to acknowledge it and validate it. You deserve tender care.

When I became disabled at twenty-six, I forfeited the option to feign wellness. My hurts are displayed across my paralyzed face and tremoring arm and unsteady gait. For me, there's no pretending that everything is okay. And what a profound blessing that has proven to be. I wish I hadn't waited to acknowledge my fragility until a stroke did it for me. Owning my fragility brought me to a place of freedom and overwhelming empathy. Now I can never fool myself into treating anyone with carelessness or callousness because I know they are sitting in a wheelchair of their own, even if it's invisible. Every last one of us deserves the grace of the assumption that all is not well.

Not one of us is fully able, no matter how typically—or even ideally—our bodies and brains function. Think about it. Do you always feel fully free, even if you can walk on your own? Do you always feel truly beautiful, even if your face is not paralyzed? Do you always feel completely understood, even without a speech impairment? The answer, of course, is a resounding no. We all are disabled. Some of our "wheelchairs" are simply on the inside instead of the outside.

This truth inspires me to treat other people with immense tenderness and to extend that same care to myself. However, it also reminds me that each of us is braver and more resilient than we realize. If we're navigating an unkind world from the seats of our physical or invisible wheelchairs, we are pretty darn strong *because* of our weaknesses. Recognizing that paradoxical miracle has transformed the way I see the purpose in my pain.

If it's true for me, could it be true for you too?

OWNING MY INNER FRAGILITY CAN BRING ME
TO A PLACE OF FREEDOM AND EMPATHY.

17

DUSTY

Much of the old to-do list goes neglected when you're a disabled, working parent who can't drive. But I feel no small amount of pride to report that Jay and I recently updated and signed our wills, since the last version was about ten years, one cross-country move, and a second child out of date.

Of all days, the signing happened on Ash Wednesday. As I stared at my stroke-affected signature scrawled across the printed will on that first day of Lent, I felt the full force of my mortality. It might as well have been a hand-delivered invitation from God to remember my humanness.

I can't recognize my humanness without also recognizing that (1) to be human is to be not-God, (2) I'm headed toward the grave, and (3) there is going to be a lot of regret (and hopefully repentance) along the way.

In short: I'm going from dust to dust with a lot of mess in between. That's the human experience, squeezed onto the page of a will and revealed in the smudge of ash on a forehead.

In our younger years, remembering our mortality feels a lot like paying for health insurance. In theory, you understand it's a useful thing to do. But in reality, you're young! You're invincible! You still have all your teeth! Why would you consider (much less pay for) a hypothetical time when that may change?

But then you have a stroke. Or you lose a spouse on what should have been an ordinary day. Or a cancer moves into your body without asking permission. At some point, recognizing our mortality becomes painfully, critically relevant, whether we like it or not.

With each day that I move further from the beginning of my life and nearer to the end, I feel more and more human. That is to say, I feel more and more like dust. My beat-up, half-functioning body reminds me multiple times an hour just how fallible and finite I am. And my fragile spirit—still so vulnerable to fear and despair and pride—reminds me just how not-God I am. And these reminders—these memento mori—are a gift given by the darkness. They draw me toward dependence rather than dread.

I've grazed death so closely that I can still feel it on my fingertips. That experience left me with no other choice but to cling to the hope of a reality deeper than this one. The dust of my life may not always be beautiful or tidy, but it has been fertile soil for God to grow humility and gratitude and faithfulness.

Resisting our humanity serves us in no way. Whether we acknowledge it or not, our busted-up dustiness is a fact. Instead of sweeping it into a corner of our consciousness or collapsing in a hopeless pile of ashes, I want to believe my life can be a little garden plot where Divine Love might choose to grow good fruit on my journey from dust to dust.

If it's true for me, could it be true for you too?

MY HUMANITY PROVIDES FERTILE SOIL FOR GOD TO
GROW HUMILITY, GRATITUDE, AND FAITHFULNESS.

18

THE SUFFERING QUOTA

If you're reading this book, you probably have released the notion of anything resembling a "prosperity gospel" long ago, if you ever believed in it in the first place. Suffering will do that for you. It's like a comically timed, open-palmed slap across the face. *Smack.* Any experience of suffering will shock us out of believing God's will is simple, straightforward "wellness" or "prosperity." For me, suffering has upended just about every definition in the dictionary of my life, *wellness* included.

After surviving my capital-S Season of Suffering, I must have assumed the mandatory trauma box for my life had been ticked with a big red check mark. *Thanks, God! Lesson learned. So glad that's over so we can focus on thriving now, rather than just surviving.*

But once I'd cleared the thickest stretches of my stroke recovery, something mystifying occurred: Hard things kept happening. And happening. And happening.

Like, seriously?! Are you as *appalled* as I was?

Multiple aneurysms were discovered in my brain. I've obliterated my right leg not once but twice, because of flukish falls. My father was diagnosed with aggressive multiple myeloma as my sister continued an exhausting battle with addiction. Then I developed life-threatening dissections in my vertebral artery that put me on the edge of another stroke. And that was all by my fortieth birthday!

It didn't take long to recognize I'd subscribed to a sequel of the prosperity gospel. I had believed there was a built-in limit on hardship. But after experiencing a few lifetimes' worth of pain in a single decade of adulthood, I got the message loud and clear: there is no quota on suffering. I wish someone had told me sooner, which is why I'm telling you!

No matter the number of hard days you have behind you, not one of us is guaranteed an exemption from even harder days ahead. This inspires anything but hope. Suffering not only saturates the present with pain; it also reaches forward and fills the future with danger and dread. We learn that if a bad thing has happened, it can happen again. Maybe even worse next time.

Before you give up altogether, I have good news. That line of reasoning can be inverted if you're brave enough to flip it around: If a good thing has happened, then it can happen again. Maybe even better.

After enduring countless major and minor stints of suffering since my stroke, I've conditioned myself to identify opportunities for hope, rather than hopelessness, within my circumstances. Yes, my life has been—and will be—full of hard things. But it's also been absolutely overflowing with good things, which means the future is full of good things if I am willing to recognize them. While my suffering has no quota, neither does my hope.

If it's true for me, could it be true for you too?

LIFE IS FULL OF HARD THINGS, BUT IT'S ALSO FULL OF GOOD THINGS. THIS MEANS THE FUTURE IS FULL OF GOOD THINGS IF I AM WILLING TO RECOGNIZE THEM.

19

IN SEASON

Raised in the Deep South and seasoned with fifteen years of young adulthood in Southern California, I am a bona fide warm-weather, thin-blooded, sunshine-loving human being. I've survived so much, but every winter, I wonder if the cold might finally take me down. Apparently, I've passed this on to my sons, whom Jay and I call our little "grannies" because of their habit of watching movies in front of a space heater while being wrapped in blankets and robes in our centrally heated home in famously hot Atlanta, Georgia.

I'm still not a fan of the cold, but life, with its wily ways of cracking open old beliefs, has revealed to me that every season serves a function. Yes, even winter. (Eye roll.)

In November 2020, I was trying out a new adaptive bicycle during a family loop around our neighborhood and accidentally steered off a curb. I tumbled with the bike and badly tore the "unholy trinity" of my ACL, MCL, and meniscus. I was all but bedridden for months. In hopes of making the funk a bit more festive, I listened to multiple audiobooks on the concept of *hygge* (pronounced *hoo-guh*; you're welcome!). This Danish philosophy embraces the opportunities for coziness and comfort exclusive to the winter months. Beyond giving us a flimsy-at-best excuse to chow down on hearty stews with abandon and wear our bathrobes for days on end, *hygge* redefines even the coldest and darkest seasons by focusing on what they make available, not what they take away.

If you're like me, you might tend to avoid, resist, or altogether deny the not-so-sunny seasons. We numb ourselves so we don't feel the chill as deeply. We might try a quick fix for those wounds that only time can heal. Or, like our old neighbors in

California during the single day of rainy weather each year, we might even get angry, thrust a fist into the air, and proclaim, "This is not what I signed up for and not what I deserve!"

I'm not an expert on much, but I've learned a thing or two about squeezing every good thing I can out of the season in front of me. I've seen beauty and utility in them all. I really like the heart behind *hygge* because it acknowledges that although the winter can be hard, it's the time when roots grow deeper and stronger. This is the great possibility offered by our own winters too.

In our interior climates, dark winter seasons of the soul can be a time to store up patience, grit, and grace. Hope is believing the seeds of spiritual practices and remembrance of God's goodness will blossom at the right time. Most of the best fruit in my life was incubated in dark, cold seasons of suffering. Today I'm thankful for the fruit of Hope Heals Camp and Mend Coffee & Goods—my treasured communities of thousands of people affected by disabilities—that grew from the soil of my life's worst moments. For you, some long-awaited fruit may be ready to enjoy this very day. Or perhaps new roots are invisibly incubating in the silence and stillness of your suffering. Either way, your season is serving the larger story.

Whether I'm hunkered down in the harshest winter of my life or relishing the most gorgeous spring I could imagine, I want to dig my heels into the good/hard reality of the climate I'm in. I've tasted and seen that growing good fruit requires enduring dark seasons.

If it's true for me, could it be true for you too?

SOME OF THE BEST FRUIT IN MY LIFE WILL BE INCUBATED
IN DARK, COLD SEASONS OF SUFFERING.

20

NO PAIN, NO GAIN

Before my stroke, I was a working model and actress. After my stroke, I became a full-time therapy patient. Astoundingly, that gig paid even less than my entertainment industry work! But I did become one of the best in the business, if I do say so myself. From swallowing and speech therapy to physical and occupational therapy to emotional therapy, I did it all. I retrained my mouth to form words, built up my balance to walk again in a new way, put in hours and hours in the gym to strengthen my core, and spent two afternoons a week at the community pool to work on limb coordination.

A solid decade of regular therapies helped me find a new way of navigating the world with security and creativity. Almost none of it was fun, and every bit of it was hard. If you've ever been prescribed physical therapy for an injury, you know as well as I do that the results require a certain amount of discomfort, and maybe even a little bit of straight-up pain! More than once, I've restrained myself from reflexively punching a physical therapist when she stretches a limb a titch too far. I'm more of a lover than a fighter, and my hand isn't coordinated enough to actually land the punch, but the sentiment remains!

In the midst of our cross-country move from Los Angeles to Atlanta in 2018, I paused my decade-long therapy routines. Then, in the midst of settling into a full new life in a new city, the routines went altogether dormant. Suddenly, over two years of life had passed without a single hour of formal therapy.

After my ligament-obliterating fall in 2020, I was immobilized for several weeks until the swelling subsided enough for surgery. Then, just days after the operation, I was enrolled in an intensive physical therapy regimen before I could even get out of bed on my own. Although the incisions were still fresh and I could feel the newly installed ligaments and pins every time I moved my leg, the surgeon insisted I get to work immediately. So, with some choice words in mind for my physician, I reluctantly got started.

It took nine months of grueling, teeth-gritting effort, but bit by bit, I progressed from total immobility back to my poststroke baseline. Eventually, I even reached a level of physical stability and agility I never had attained in my years of being disabled. All the stretching and straining and suffering ended up strengthening me. I enjoyed exactly zero seconds of the whole ordeal, but I can't deny the results.

I think our longing to enjoy gentleness and ease in life is a healthy one; we are designed to crave beauty over brokenness. To suffer for suffering's sake would make me a certifiable psychopath. But I never want to miss an opportunity for my pain to become gain because I'm unwilling to struggle for a while. My experiences of physical and occupational therapies have proven to me that bodily strength develops when I stretch a little deeper or stand a little longer or swim a little farther than I thought I could. My story of suffering has taught me that soul strength develops when we keep showing up to the lives in front of us, even when the pain and disappointment feel like more than we can bear.

I wonder if there is a pain of yours that is inviting you into growth today.

The breaking of my heart became the making of who I really am—of who I was always meant to be. Maybe the truest, strongest *you* is waiting on the other side of the breaking. So maybe I don't have to resist it anymore, and neither do you. Just like the firing of clay, the tanning of leather, or the breaking down and building up of muscles, pain can be a crucial part of our progress toward resilience and refinement if we let it be.

If it's true for me, could it be true for you too?

PAIN CAN BE A CRUCIAL PART OF MY PROGRESS
TOWARD RESILIENCE AND REFINEMENT.

21

NOT THE SAME

I am the same on the inside. I am the same on the inside. I am the same on the inside.

I couldn't speak yet. Just over two months before, my stroke had left me unable to vocalize a single word. The surgery that saved my life had also decimated almost every one of my fundamental abilities.

When I made the move from the intensive care unit to an acute neurological rehab floor, I was given an electronic letter board like some strange graduation gift in this awful parallel-universe version of my life. Hungry for an outlet for the billion thoughts and questions dammed up inside my mind, I just about wore the buttons off that letter board once I got my hands on it.

My face and body were unrecognizable to me and to everyone who knew me. I couldn't do anything or say anything or eat anything. But I was desperate to assure the people around me that I was still Katherine. My mind, personality, cognition, and faith were totally intact. With everything I had, I was grasping for the baseline of who I'd been. Nearly obsessively, I used the index finger of my left hand, which hadn't been affected by my stroke, to type out: I AM STILL THE SAME ON THE INSIDE.

I understand why I needed to communicate this message. It was true in many ways, of course. But now, over fifteen years later, I can say that I am not the same on the inside. Just about everything within me has changed. And I'm not grasping for that old baseline anymore.

After my stroke, Jay and I spent months waiting for our reality to stop spinning long enough to catch our balance. Once we did, we spent years attempting to recreate the lives we'd been living and the people we had been before everything changed. Bless us. We were truly convinced we'd be able to casually sneak in the back door of our old lives. But our old lives simply did not fit us anymore.

Until my stroke, I understood suffering as something to be avoided at all costs. And if I couldn't avoid it, then I should get through it as quickly as possible and pretend it never happened. No one had ever told me that my pain could be the most powerful and positive agent of change in my life, if I chose to let it be. Suffering doesn't have to be the end of the story. It can be the beginning of a new story. A new baseline. A new me and a new you.

After years of faithful prayer from friends around the world, I made considerable progress physically. (I also put in a lot of work too. Imagine a version of the *Rocky* training montage, starring me!) But I never leaped from my wheelchair like I had dreamed—and expected—that I would. My outside is drastically different now, yes. But my mind and soul are different too. If I could do it all again, I'd waste less time resisting what was different and new. I'd surrender my longing to stay the same so I could receive the new life being offered to me. Maintaining the status quo doesn't have to be my highest good anymore.

If you're desperate to hang on to the sameness in your life, instead get curious about what new thing your suffering could be offering to you. Maybe it's a soul-deep contentment distinct from desired outcomes. Maybe it's a capacity for greater trust because you've known such great loss. Or maybe it's a total overhaul of your priorities. If you ask me, becoming new is starting to sound a heck of a lot better than staying the same.

God is making all things new, and that includes you and me. Because of the transforming hope of God, I am stronger, softer, and more surrendered than I ever knew I could be. I am not the same on the inside. And thank God for that.

If it's true for me, could it be true for you too?

MAINTAINING THE STATUS QUO DOESN'T HAVE
TO BE MY HIGHEST GOOD ANYMORE.

For me, a run-of-the-mill trip to the grocery store or park usually includes a few wide-eyed children asking, "What's wrong with you?" or offering the ever insightful, "Your face looks weird." I've heard that kids say the darndest things, but I'm still not exactly sure what that means. After fifteen years of receiving unsolicited kiddo commentary on my paralyzed face, I'm beginning to think that saying is a euphemism for "Kids have the power to devastate your self-image in four words flat."

Little ones let it fly most freely, but expectations about how our bodies should look come from every direction. Be thin, be strong, be able-bodied, and—for the love of Botox—be young! This is what it takes to be loved and to belong. But there's a quieter, more insidious voice whispering what a good life should look like: be unbroken, no matter what's happened to you.

And this is not just physical. It's in the ways we act as if we haven't been shattered inside. The difficult reality is that we are not always complicit in our own shattering. Sure, some brokenness stems from consequences of our own unwise choices. More often, trauma and the resulting fractures are imposed on us from the outside. And even when we bear little or no responsibility for our wounds, the experiences of hurt leave us saddled with overwhelming shame.

Logically, we know that we don't deserve the shame. But our deepest parts still feel where the trauma has broken us, and that brokenness diminishes our peace, joy, and confidence. We're disqualified from the world's narrative of a good life because we are smaller now, less than whole.

Traumas—both big and small—should never be ignored or repressed. In the right time, they should be confronted and processed in the safety of trusted friends or professional counselors or both. As I've undertaken the hard work of engaging the injuries to my spirit, one question has been indispensable to my healing: What if I chose to approach trauma as an expansion of myself rather than as a diminishing?

Jesus said it this way: "Unless a grain of wheat is buried in the ground, dead to the world, it is never any more than a grain of wheat. But if it is buried, it sprouts and reproduces itself many times over. In the same way, anyone who holds on to life just as it is destroys that life. But if you let it go, reckless in your love, you'll have it forever, real and eternal" (John 12:24–25 MSG).

Trauma can break open our hearts and minds to make room for something more full, complex, and fruitful than the little wheat kernel of "wholeness" we had before we were hurt. When we recognize that trauma is a type of death—the death of dreams, innocence, independence, or security—it then becomes an opportunity for resurrection.

Resurrection, the ultimate beauty, is predicated on death. And death is the ultimate trauma. Fortunately, we know a God who refuses to let trauma have the last word. In fact, that's kind of His whole deal. He repurposes our brokenness into beauty through remaking and resurrecting. We see it in the Christ story and in our own second-chance stories. He allows us to be buried so we can sprout into something new.

There's more goodness to be found in the depth and resilience of my resurrected life than in an existence that's never needed healing. There's more sacred beauty, I think, in a face that's been scarred than in one without flaw. In a body that's been healed than in one without blemish. In a soul that's been broken open than in one that's intact but closed up. This kind of beauty has to be discovered and developed. But, goodness, is it worth the effort.

If it's true for me, could it be true for you too?

I CAN CHOOSE TO APPROACH TRAUMA AS AN EXPANSION
OF MYSELF RATHER THAN AS A DIMINISHING.

23

WAKE-UP CALL

Where am I?

My eyes roved my fluorescent-lit surroundings, which appeared in my vision as two blurry hospital rooms doubled over one another. My gaze landed on Jay (or two Jays, really), who was sitting in a blue vinyl chair in the corner. I tried to call out to him, but my throat couldn't produce a sound.

What had happened to me?

A full two and a half months was—and still is—missing from my brain's record. From the moment of my collapse on the afternoon of April 21, 2008, until early July, I was not an active participant in my own life. Then, as the dense fog of semiconsciousness began to lift, I started the bewildering process of "waking up" to my new normal. My brain worked overtime to understand that I no longer lived in our on-campus law school apartment and that our baby, James—who was suddenly months older—could only visit my hospital room during certain hours of the day. I tried to compute that I could "eat" only through a plastic tube in my belly and that my mouth couldn't form words I wanted to say, no matter how hard I tried to enunciate. How could my entire life have been as tenuous as a tangled blood vessel?

I was waking up physically, sure. But I was also waking up in a much deeper way. Until my stroke, I had lived in a sort of charmed spiritual semiconsciousness, lulled into the dreamy illusion that I had some meaningful control over the way things would unfold for me. But in reality, my body, brain, and future were more fragile than I ever dared to imagine.

In that sterile, white hospital room, I was waking up to my specific reality, yes, but I was also waking up to an expansive, universal reality: life is unspeakably delicate. This had always been the case, but my stroke forced me to acknowledge the fact that every plan, security, assumption, foregone conclusion, and ability can change in an instant.

And, friend, my situation is not an exception. It's the rule. Whether you know it or not, your life is as fragile as mine. Maybe you've already received the unwanted wake-up call to the tissue-thin tenuousness of your charmed life. Or maybe the alarm is getting ready to sound. Coming to terms with our frailty could send us hiding under the bedcovers in fear or drive us mad with worry. Or, it could reveal that, because life is more breakable than we ever knew, every day is more miraculous than we ever acknowledged.

Surviving didn't make my life miraculous; it merely uncovered the miracle that was already there. After all, even if I'd never had the stroke, I would still be living an unlikely, undeserved miracle of a life. I just wouldn't know it.

I really do believe we can thank God for our wake-up calls, no matter how painful they may be, because they invite us to live differently. To live with whole hearts and open hands. Once we know how simultaneously frail and fantastic we really are, we can't help but revel in the graces of our second-chance lives like the undeserved gifts that they are. When you're awake, no day goes unappreciated. No provision goes unnoticed. No lesson goes unlearned.

When our lives fall apart again (because, spoiler alert, they will), the brittle breaking won't have to hurt quite as badly. Now that I'm awake to the reality of my life, I won't be startled into consciousness the next time my world is shattered. I'm finally living like the miracle I've always been—weak and wonderful, all at once.

If it's true for me, could it be true for you too?

ONCE I KNOW HOW SIMULTANEOUSLY FRAIL AND
FANTASTIC I REALLY AM, I CAN LIVE MY SECOND-CHANCE
LIFE WITH A WHOLE HEART AND OPEN HANDS.

24

HITTING THE LIMITS

In the modern age, and particularly in the Western world, we value personal freedom more dearly than almost any other principle. Living within limitations can feel like an inconvenience, if not an outright injustice. We strain toward a promised land of self-determination, fully buying into the health, wealth, and happiness to which we are so clearly entitled. A stroke, of all things, cured me of this particular illusion.

Too many people on earth live under very real and deeply inequitable restrictions, the kind of restrictions that *all* of us should push against as we work to build God's kingdom. Others among us—myself included—enjoy an abundance of freedom, yet still manage to twist the best things in our lives until they look like limitations. We buy into the narratives that our kids stole our free time or our spouses stunted our personal growth. Our jobs aren't fulfilling enough (despite the reliable paycheck), and our bodies won't cooperate with our ill-conceived ideals of beauty.

I'm not scolding anyone here, believe me. I've thrown my share of toddler-style tantrums (on the inside . . . usually) fueled by the frustration of not being able to drive or walk independently or feel the coffee dripping from the paralyzed corner of my mouth (and onto yet another ruined white shirt. Sorry, Jay!). Even after becoming disabled, I still find myself opting into a system where autonomy and ability are considered requirements for fulfillment. I'm working to separate myself and my family from this flawed operation every single day. But living with disabilities has transformed the way I understand Jesus. My impression of Him has progressed beyond the glorified Victor and Overcomer, whose life among people was just a means to the end of resurrection.

Jesus' experience on earth was defined by living *within* limitations, not transcending them. (Sounds like you and me, doesn't it?) The eternal, universal force of Christ was squeezed into a human womb and constrained by the body of a baby. He was limited to communicating with human language, lived alongside small-minded and small-spirited people, and then died under unjust pretenses. If I were the Son of God and had been dealt that hand, I would have requested a reassignment, ASAP.

As a person living with pretty considerable disabilities, I now understand that knowing the earthbound Jesus, with all His limitations, is as meaningful as knowing the risen-again Christ. Within all His constraints, Jesus not only flourished but lived the single most extraordinary life imaginable. It may sound odd, but I truly think that Jesus disabled Himself by becoming a man. When He did it, He dignified my disabilities and limitations. And He dignified yours too.

Beauty and goodness thrive when we trace the boundary lines God has drawn for us and choose to call them pleasant (Psalm 16:6). The only limitation we should bust out of is the *limiting* theology of boundless autonomy and self-determination.

Life with disabilities has shown me how my weak parts and worst failures create open spaces where miracles can spring up. My limitations today are mere shadows of the ultimate limitation: death. And death was exactly the limitation Jesus used to work out our path to new life. I believe thriving in limitations is possible. Not just for Jesus but for me too.

If it's true for me, could it be true for you too?

IF JESUS' EXPERIENCE ON EARTH WAS ABOUT LIVING WITHIN LIMITATIONS, NOT TRANSCENDING THEM, MINE CAN BE TOO.

SHOWING UP SCARED

Poked, prodded, injected, anesthetized, transfused, incised, stitched, monitored, and shocked. I've clocked in for thirteen surgeries, dozens of treatments, and hundreds of therapy sessions since my stroke. (In retrospect, some kind of punch card system would have been nice!) Oddly enough, the medical to-do that I dread most doesn't require a single incision and is (technically) painless: the MRI.

A brain MRI requires patients to lie completely still—head immobilized—inside a long, plastic cylinder as radio waves produce images of the brain. Over the last fifteen years, I've had more of these scans than I can count. To this day, my feet still tingle and my hands go a bit numb as I sit in the waiting room before a scheduled MRI. The scans can last up to an hour and a half, which feels like a week and a half when you're the one entombed inside that cold tube.

I get a pit in my stomach when I imagine the claustrophobia of an MRI machine. If I look deep inside that pit, I see that my fear is not really about the tight space. I'm actually most afraid of what new bad thing might show up on the scan. Another aneurysm? More vertebral dissections? Some fresh new neurovascular abnormality that will threaten my life yet again? I'm a little scared of the process of getting an MRI, sure. But I'm most intimidated by the reality that, as long as I have breath in my lungs, new hardships will continue to show up and demand my engagement.

Jay has accompanied me to every single scan and doctor's appointment and therapy session and we'll-try-anything-once alternative medicine treatment. While he's not allowed to sit in the room with me during an MRI, he always takes a seat alongside the technician in the adjacent control room and rigs up a perfectly curated classical music playlist for me to listen to through the piped-in speakers. During a recent scan, my nerves were particularly frazzled and my edginess failed to soften during the entire ninety-minute ordeal. I couldn't make my hands stop shaking, even though I had been instructed to lie perfectly still. *Will this ever get easier?* I found myself wondering during the long silence.

Inside that machine, I felt afraid of the future and exhausted by what it would require of me. I thought doing hard things over and over again would make them get less hard. But sometimes they don't get any easier. Often, they just get harder.

Maybe that's kind of the point, I thought while I was inside the tube. Maybe this good/hard life is less about ease and more about showing up scared to the ongoing hard with ongoing hope. It's not about life hurting less; it's about our hearts hoping more. I can accept the reality that hard things are ahead, then I can decide to show up to my life, no matter how scared I may feel. And while I'm at it, I'll praise God through the whole hard process because He is showing up too. Right there beside me. Do you ever look to the life ahead of you only to see opportunities for more suffering?

My MRI epiphany was interrupted by a loud beeping. The scan was finally complete. The technician slid me out from the machine, and in a swell of serendipity, Jay's playlist shuffled to Handel's "Hallelujah" chorus.

Hallelujah, indeed. Maybe hands shaking in fear are as good as hands raised in praise. Life will probably never get easier for any of us, but is ease what we really want at the end of it all? I want to continue showing up scared, and I want to continue praising God in—and for—this heck of a hard and holy process.

If it's true for me, could it be true for you too?

THE GOOD/HARD LIFE IS LESS ABOUT EASE AND
MORE ABOUT SHOWING UP SCARED TO THE ONGOING
HARD AND CHOOSING ONGOING HOPE.

26

A LOW-GRADE SORROW

When my husband and son lost me, I was alive to watch the whole thing happen. At least, that's sure how it felt. Every privilege and responsibility of my role as a wife and mom was snatched away in a matter of minutes. By God's grace, Jay and James were well cared for by a concerned village as I slowly rose from the dead. Surrounded by a robust fan club of family and friends, my baby did not suffer from lack of attention as he experienced many of his milestone firsts.

I was neither conscious nor present for most of those firsts. In fact, I wasn't even awake for many of my own first experiences of motherhood. My first Mother's Day was spent in the ICU. After nearly three months, I began regaining consciousness and my cognition clarified a bit. But my broader situation did not improve. I was simply more in tune with all the things I wasn't able to do with and for James. Sometimes in that season, James looked at me without a trace of recognition in his eyes. I felt as if I had become irrelevant to him.

The first few years after my stroke, James and I physically progressed at roughly the same pace—learning to walk, talk, eat, and write in stride with one another. It was kind of cute but mostly kind of sad. As I grew stronger and he grew more independent, we reached a sort of rhythm that partially satisfied my longing to be his mom once again.

Years later, after my doctors gave me their blessing to try to have another baby, my hopes for second-chance motherhood grew as big as my pregnant belly. I was convinced God would use this new life to redeem my near-death. I just knew the weight of my grief would finally be lifted once the baby arrived and I got a chance at a do-over. I placed my hope for healing on the tiny shoulders of an unborn baby. Real healthy, I know.

John Wolf's arrival blessed me with a surge of fresh purpose, delight, and hope. Six months into my second-chance motherhood, John's firsts became true firsts for me, too, as he began hitting the milestones that James had reached while I lay semiconscious in an intensive care unit. But it didn't take long to realize that raising this beloved second child was failing to undo the damage done by *not* raising my first child. Those first years of motherhood would never be returned to me. I began to understand that even if I had a dozen more babies and regained every one of my lost abilities, I'd never feel totally whole again.

The book of Ecclesiastes makes the fascinating, maddening observation that although God has "set eternity in the human heart," we'll never be able to grasp exactly what He's doing from beginning to end (3:11). We all know deep down how the story is supposed to end, but we don't know precisely how He's going to pull it off. That space between the knowing and the not knowing is where a low-grade sorrow pulses, in my heart and in yours. It's a sorrow that will always be with us, as some of our losses will remain, even in the midst of so much restoration. Some of our hurts will be healed only by heaven.

Whenever that makes our hearts ache, I think we can use the sadness as a reminder that there is something beyond this present pain. So when we feel the residual desperation for resolution, we don't have to lose hope.

I'm still feeling the ache these days, even as I sit front-row for every moment and milestone of my sons' lives. But I'm thankful for the ache because it's proof of a someday restoration we are designed and destined to experience. The ache tells me the shade of healing I've received on this side of heaven will deepen into something absolutely whole. The ache tells me I will be healed.

If it's true for me, could it be true for you too?

NO MATTER HOW MUCH HEALING I RECEIVE, A LOW-GRADE SADNESS WILL REMAIN. IT'S AN ACHE THAT IS PROOF OF THE WHOLENESS I AM DESIGNED TO EXPERIENCE.

27

FACING DEATH AGAIN

It was 2017 and I was nine years past my life-changing stroke. An almost two-year-old John, my miracle baby, toddled around the living room as I watched from my seat on the couch. I held a mug of coffee in my hand that had gone cold yet again, despite having been nuked three times already. Even though it was only eight o'clock on a Sunday morning, the coffee had been brewed hours before because toddlers, by all accounts, exist to disprove the phrase "easy like Sunday morning." I was trying to kill an hour entertaining John before it was time to get ready for church.

For several weeks I'd been dealing with some weird neck pain, dull yet persistent. We'd spent the day before in typical Wolf fashion, crisscrossing Los Angeles on several personal and professional missions, including a video shoot and a family date to the movies. I figured my light-headedness that morning was just an unfortunate mix of exhaustion and dehydration. Nearly a decade into my recovery, I was finally able to carefully hobble around my house on foot, so I stood up from the couch (much too quickly, I would find out) to make my way into the kitchen. The next thing I knew, I was lying face-first on the living room carpet. I had blacked out and nose-dived forward, my body as stiff as a felled tree. The mug of cold coffee had been flung across the room and splattered all over the floor and little John. Jay immediately appeared and scooped me up.

Instead of spending the morning at church, we spent twelve maddening hours being shuffled around an emergency department. After several scans, we were told everything looked fine and the episode had just been a blood pressure fluke. Deeply relieved, we returned home to our boys and crawled into bed.

In the early hours of the next morning, my phone rang. A doctor had taken a second look at my scans and discovered multiple vertebral artery dissections, or what we would become accustomed to calling VADs. I was on the verge of another stroke as blood flow to my brain was blocked. We returned to the hospital for five terrible days and found ourselves with an excruciating amount of free time to consider what could be ahead.

Will I have another stroke? I wondered obsessively. *There's no way someone survives two strokes before they're forty, right? What if the dissections keep appearing? Can I handle being even more disabled than I already am?*

But somewhere around the thousandth orbit of the same thoughts around my brain, I realized something obvious: *Earth to Katherine! You already survived the very worst day of your life. And about a thousand runner-up worst days. You can do this because you've already done it.*

In that moment, my fear of the unknown suffering ahead did not disappear altogether, but it did shrink to a manageable size. I could face the future with the confidence of someone who had already survived her past. I'd survived once, and nothing could take that from me.

Even if your situation isn't quite as dramatic as mine, the truth remains: every hard day of your life has prepared you for the hardest day of your life. Maybe you're in a practice round. Or maybe you are finally putting all that hard-won practice to use. Either way, you can face the day in front of you with the confidence of someone who has trained.

I left my stay in the hospital with a brutal blood-thinning regimen and instructions to treat myself like a porcelain doll . . . or maybe it was a Fabergé egg? It would take my medical team years (and two more VADs) to discover the root cause of the dissections. As you know by now, it turns out I have a rare, unnamed neurovascular disorder that will likely cause me issues for the rest of my life. Now, I pop a baby aspirin every single day to prevent more dissections and clots.

It may sound counterintuitive, but I'm convinced that the immense loss wreaked by my stroke actually brought me to a place of deep freedom and preparedness. I am the same person who survived the worst day, and God is the same God who was with me through it all. The unexpected gift of facing death—or loss or disappointment or doubt—means feeling a bit more prepared to face it, or something else hard, again. If it's true for me, could it be true for you too?

EVERY HARD DAY OF MY LIFE HAS PREPARED ME
FOR THE NEXT HARDEST DAY OF MY LIFE.

A REUNION

While I am a girl's girl, I am decidedly not a *girls' weekend* girl. But last winter I was invited to a girls' weekend I couldn't turn down: the twenty-five-year class reunion for Camp DeSoto, the beloved all-girls camp I attended every summer of my childhood and adolescence. To say I'm obsessed with Camp DeSoto would be the understatement of the century. In the no-filter-on-my-mouth season of brain rehab, I was asked what the best day of my life had been. Without hesitation (and to Jay's eye-rolling horror), I responded, "The day I led my team to win the Final Cup at my last year of Camp DeSoto!" Needless to say, I immediately RSVPed *yes* to the reunion.

The get-together was happening in Atlanta where I live, but I still counted it as my first poststroke solo trip—even if Jay dropped me off and picked me up like a twelve-year-old going to a sleepover. Most of us in the group hadn't been in the same room together since we were sixteen years old, so I anticipated hours of laughter and lighthearted catching up. What I got instead was harder but so much better.

Our first night together, we were each given a poster board and marker, then allotted half an hour to "teach" the rest of the group about the last twenty-five years of our lives. One by one, each woman stood up (although I got a pass on the standing requirement) and told the story of her life since Camp DeSoto—where she had gone to college, if and who she'd married, what career she'd chosen, and how many kids she had.

Beyond the standard biographical stuff, every woman also shared her experiences of life-defining hardship. Our suffering took the forms of divorce, infertility, unwanted singleness, unfaithful spouses, deaths of parents, critical medical diagnoses, spiritual abuse . . . and even a stroke. What started as a fun exercise ended in stunned but cathartic tears, our hearts broken for each other and for ourselves.

Not one woman in that room was living the life she'd imagined when she was a girl at summer camp. And I imagine you aren't either. In fact, I think to be human is to live in the space between our expectations and reality. The space where hopes and dreams are powerless to tame life's chaos. The space called *suffering*. Of course, our expectations aren't bad in themselves, but the way we orient ourselves around them can make or break our experience of life and our relationship with God. So what should we do with all these expectations? The answer is simple but so hard to pull off: expect more of God and less of the world.

The next morning of the reunion, I led our throwback vespers service. Together, we sang some of our favorite camp songs from memory. The words fell out effortlessly:

> *When you pass through the waters, I will be with you*
> *And through rivers, they will not overwhelm you*
> *When you walk through the fire, you will not be burned*
> *The flames shall not consume you*
> *Fear not, for I have redeemed you*
> *I have called you by name. You are mine.*[3]

I reflected out loud how this and other songs had comforted us as little girls even though we hadn't really understood them then. Now, halfway through life, we finally knew what they had been saying all along: When the world abandons you, God is with you. When the world disappoints you, God makes a way. When the world rejects you, God calls you by name. Expect more of God and less of the world.

That's why these women were still standing. Still breathing. They had traded their expectations that the world would fulfill them for expectations that God would sustain them. This didn't mean they entirely understood their God—but, goodness, did they trust Him. And so can I. So can you.

If it's true for me, could it be true for you too?

I CAN EXPECT MORE OF GOD AND LESS OF THE WORLD.

29

THE WORST DAY

Some days of the year are not created equal.

When springtime reaches its fullness near the end of April—the twenty-first of April, to be exact—my soul deflates a little, without fail. Reminders of death flood my mind and senses, crowding out the beauty of the season. Just as nature hits its annual high note of new life, I'm forced to remember the day I almost died.

The sights and sounds and sensations of April 21, 2008, are burned into my mind with sharp-edged clarity. I can taste the bile in the back of my throat as nausea overtook me. I can smell the ground beef that was simmering on the stove when I collapsed on the kitchen floor. I can hear Jay screaming my name with a panic in his voice I'd never heard before.

It was the worst day of my life, and I assume it ranks near the bottom for the people who love me. Despite the slow-motion "resurrection" that was to come, so many things died to me on April 21.

We all have *that day* that changed everything. That day that ripped through our stories and left a line of demarcation between the life we now have and the one we will never get back. And the anniversaries of those days—which have the audacity to roll around every single year!—guarantee we are never able to forget what we've lost.

Three years into my recovery, Holy Week coincided with the anniversary of my stroke. This intersection left me with a complicated emotional surplus, to put it delicately. You could say I had some feedback for God. Still deep in the grief of the loss of my old life, I was more in the Good Friday mindset than the Resurrection Day spirit. The narrative of hope didn't seem to belong to me.

But when I continued to take in the story of Jesus that Holy Week, God whispered a fresh narrative of hope. He handed me a new way of framing my story, and it changed everything.

If the worst day of Jesus' life was eventually called *good*, then maybe one day my worst day would be called *good* too.

Jesus' second-chance life gave me permission to hope that good things could come from my hard story. Now I can see resurrection instead of just death in the place where one life ends and a new one begins. I'm being made more alive and more complete by the very thing that should have killed me; I have joined the story of Jesus, the story of hope. He hasn't erased my pain, but He sure has redeemed it.

As signs of spring continue to appear year after year, my stomach will still flutter and my heart will still feel a bit heavier than usual. And you know what? That's okay. My worst day will remain my worst day. But I've already lived to see that day be called *good*, which gives me enormous hope for facing all the hard days ahead of me.

If it's true for me, could it be true for you too?

IF THE WORST DAY OF JESUS' LIFE WAS EVENTUALLY CALLED *GOOD*, THEN MAYBE ONE DAY MY WORST DAY COULD BE CALLED *GOOD* TOO.

30

CONSTELLATIONS

I'm sure you'll be positively shocked to learn I'm not much of a nature person. I'm more of a "nature sounds playing over speakers in the spa" person. Yes, Jay and I founded Hope Heals Camp, a retreat experience for families living with disabilities. And yes, we technically spend a large portion of every summer living in a national forest in middle-of-nowhere Alabama. But our version of camp has air-conditioning and hot showers and acai bowls. Our friends with disabilities "rough it" in the most real sense of the phrase every single day, so we can't be convinced to rough it much during camp.

People make the pilgrimage to camp because they have suffered, not because their lives have been perfect. It's a receptacle for hundreds of the most gut-wrenching stories you could imagine. To the uninitiated, Hope Heals Camp probably sounds like a whopping bummer, an anti-vacation teeming with reminders of mortality and life's fragility. Seems pretty dark, right?

In some ways, Hope Heals Camp *is* a dark place. But if my second-chance life has taught me anything, it's that darkness can be both a heavy thing and a holy thing. Dark places can be sacred spaces, especially when they are shared.

Our little campground is nestled in a remote nook of Alabama, where the most noteworthy landmark is a gas station about fifteen miles east (with phenomenal biscuits, I might add!). Without the polluting influence of artificial lights from cities or suburbs, the expanse of night sky over camp deepens to a true black each night, and a thick dome of stars materializes overhead. The scene never fails to both soothe and astonish me as I wheel back to my cabin in the evenings.

The stars—always present, but invisible in the bright light of day—testify that some beautiful, bright things are exclusive to the darkness. I've never seen a star at high noon, after all.

Even when the sun rises each morning at Hope Heals Camp, our little gathering maintains a kind of sacred, soul-level darkness. Together, we sit in the realer-than-real pain and mystery of suffering and explore the galaxies of goodness to be found in the darkness of our stories.

We're far from the first folks to do this. For millennia, people have connected pinpricks of light in the night sky to form shapes that tell stories. At camp, we trace the lines between the spiritual stars of pain, perseverance, patience, and perspective until we can see a constellation that tells us the story of how God is making all things good. Even in the darkness. And maybe especially in the darkness.

When I return to my own backyard in light-polluted Atlanta, the stars are hard to come by and the summer's lessons are easy to forget. When the darkness of my own suffering overwhelms me, I transport myself back to the holy ground and black sky of Hope Heals Camp. I return to the sacred shadows of my co-suffering community. In my dark nights, I can map out the constellations of all the good/hard stories I've been told until I'm able to see the universe-sized shape of hope.

If it's true for me, could it be true for you too?

DARK PLACES CAN BE SACRED SPACES FOR ME,
ESPECIALLY WHEN THEY'RE SHARED.

PART TWO

FOR THE HEALING

Befriending the Lives We Have

31

THE RISK OF FAITH

Jay and I were both raised in the South, and we transplanted ourselves to Los Angeles for the first fifteen years of our adulthood. Most summers and holidays included a trip back home, which we always referred to as our "Deep-Fried Southern Tours." If you've spent even a single suppertime south of the Mason-Dixon Line, no further explanation is needed.

A Christmas visit to Jay's hometown meant a Sunday spent at the church his father had pastored for almost three decades. The congregation had followed my crisis from afar since the beginning. As we were getting our schedules sorted out for the day, my father-in-law encouraged us to visit the Katherine Wolf Prayer Meeting after the morning service. When I told him I had no idea what he was talking about, he explained that a group of men and women had gathered to pray for me every single Sunday since my stroke six years before.

Six years! Three hundred and twelve weeks! The sacrifice of this consistency and commitment put a lump in my throat. I felt humbled and honored by this gift.

A few hours later I sat in the small circle of mostly fifty-something-year-old men and women in an unused choir room and did the math on how often I had shown up to pray for my own circumstances. I needed no prompting to intercede on behalf of my son, my friends, and strangers in crisis. But talking with God about my own fears and asking for healing of my broken heart felt so much more difficult. I wanted to understand why.

In John 5, Jesus encountered a man who had suffered, bodily and socially, for decades. Jesus asked the man if he wanted to be healed. Instead of answering with a resounding, "*Duh!*" the man deflected. He hemmed and hawed and changed the subject.

Eventually, I realized that I bore a striking resemblance to my brokenhearted brother! And you might too. But really, who can blame us? Asking for a miracle is like peeling back a bandage to expose the wound that needs healing. Not one of us wants to feel vulnerable or to risk the powerlessness of not getting the outcome we desire. Faith is a risk. Praying for a miracle feels like a high-stakes gamble. (I once pulled the lever on a slot machine in the Las Vegas airport, so I speak from experience.) But Jesus continues to graciously invite us into the process. "Do you want to be healed?" He asks again.

I'm inviting you to join me in the risk of faith because, to me, it's become less about getting what I want and more about depending on Jesus. Asking Jesus to heal you is just a different way of telling Jesus, "I trust You." Praying for a miracle is not an empty gesture. It's a brave declaration of confidence in a loving God.

He is beckoning us to join Him in the miracle if we have the courage to be vulnerable. He is inviting us to believe that He will heal us at just the right time and in every way we need, even if it's not in the way we expect. And He knows something that has taken me decades to figure out: the healing starts to happen when I surrender the miracle to God's good hands and God's good plans.

If it's true for me, could it be true for you too?

IF I TAKE THE RISK OF FAITH, GOD WILL HEAL ME IN THE WAYS I NEED, EVEN IF IT'S NOT IN THE WAYS I EXPECT.

J ay recently gifted me a much-hyped fitness tracker ring. I popped it on my finger, figuring I'd occasionally use it to reach my (admittedly meager) step count
goal. But I quickly became obsessed with refreshing the stats and even found my
whole mood thrown off by a low sleep score or activity rating. Jay began calling me
Gollum and encouraged me multiple times a day to take off "my precious" ring.

What can I say? As a goal-oriented high achiever, I love forming a new habit! It's
like I'm winning the game of life. But in my well-intentioned pursuits of optimized
output and habit hacking, I have to ask myself: *What's the point of all this? Does my
lived-out reality actually sync up with my believed-in truth?*

Beyond step counts and calendar blocking and managing screen time, I want
to know how the habits of my soul can more seamlessly roll between *what* I believe
about God and *how* I practice that belief. But sometimes it's easy to confuse things
that should be practiced for things that should be believed.

I once lived as if hope were a belief, an abstraction, something that would happen
to me if I waited patiently enough. But then I survived a stroke that stranded me in
the wilderness of an intensive care unit and neuro rehab facility for years. Few places
on earth could inspire less optimism, much less a steady, sustaining hope.

I waited to feel an infusion of hope through the monotonous months of failed
swallowing tests. Saying goodbye to my family each night when visiting hours ended.
Being herded into communal showers and bathed by paid strangers. But the hope
never materialized.

The habits required by recovery became my full-time job. Not once in occupational therapy did I feel inspired to move marbles one by one with my stroke-affected

hand. A supernatural force never motivated me to make my thousandth vain attempt to choke down a teaspoonful of applesauce in swallowing therapy. But every day, I showed up and kept practicing that which had been promised to heal me.

Hope, I eventually learned, is an action. It must become a habit to be of much use. So I began practicing hope like I practiced writing or walking. I named the God I knew—the God of Purpose and Second Chances—so I could remember what to expect from Him. Like a liturgy, I recalled His faithfulness to me in the past so I could anticipate His future provision. Again and again, I affirmed what I knew to be true, even when I didn't feel it to be true: He brings beauty from ashes and turns mourning to joy (Isaiah 61:3). I didn't know when resurrection would finally happen, but I hoped and I hoped and I hoped.

No matter how uninspiring your circumstance may feel, I believe you can practice stubborn hope today. You are capable of proactively recognizing and redefining what is good in your life, here and now. You can recall and repeat God's faithfulness in your life until hope becomes a reflex.

The habit of hope carried me when the feeling of hope failed me. When I couldn't believe, I practiced instead. Now, with years and years of imperfect effort, a belief in hope has become a practiced hope that carries me through both the good and the hard.

If it's true for me, could it be true for you too?

HOPE IS SOMETHING I CAN PRACTICE, NOT
JUST SOMETHING I BELIEVE.

33

A PRAYER FOR HEALING

C an I pray for your healing?"

The question traveled through the noise of the crowded atrium, where I had the privilege of meeting with audience members after speaking at a Christian conference. People ask to pray for my healing all the time (if you use a wheelchair, you've probably had the same experience), but I couldn't stop myself from bristling at the question. I found the face of the woman who had asked to pray for me. I could tell her intentions were kind, so I collected my thoughts for a moment, then beckoned her to come closer. Jay's eyes began darting around in search of a security guard.

I have a tried-and-true method for responding in situations like these. I thank the stranger for their concern and invite them to pray for me—for God to heal my insecure heart and gossipy mouth, or for Him to protect my kids and my marriage. But before I could offer those alternative prayer topics to this particular well-meaning intercessor, she placed the entirety of her palm on my numb and paralyzed right cheek. She proceeded to whisper a prayer into my right ear, in which I am 100 percent deaf. I didn't catch a single word of it, but I suppose it didn't matter much since God was the intended audience after all.

Several minutes later she lifted her head and inspected my face. "Does it feel any different?" she asked hopefully. I half expected her to flick my cheek to see whether I could feel anything.

No, it did not feel any different. Even so, my heart softened in empathy toward this woman because my definition of healing had once been as narrow and uninspired as hers. For most of my life, before the stroke, *healing* meant being restored to an original state, and I hadn't had a reason to need it. On top of it all, I never gave much thought to whether my "original state" was worth returning to in the first place.

Now, after a decade and a half of rehabilitating my body, mind, and soul from the devastating effects of my stroke—and after years of damage incurred by simply being alive in the world—my definition of healing has blown wide-open. I've needed healing in every conceivable way and have learned that healing rarely returns us to the condition in which we started. I've also realized that my physical hurts pale in comparison to the wounds of my spirit.

My stroke created a lot of new wounds in my body. But, like any kind of suffering, it also revealed wounded parts of my soul and mind that had been hurt for a long time. While an army of faithful friends and family prayed for my physical healing— and I'm so thankful for some of my abilities that were regained because of those prayers!—I shifted my focus to the "disabilities" of my heart. I asked God to attend to my spiritual deficiencies. I prayed for a deeper capacity for empathy, a quicker willingness to forgive, and better control over my words.

I am convinced that when there's nothing to be done about what's happening on the outside, there's always room to grow stronger inside. As long as you have breath, it's never too late to push against your old definitions of healing. After all, they may not be serving you so well anymore. Once you examine the hurts in your heart with clear eyes, your physical hurts may seem a lot less dire. And healing may seem a lot more possible.

While God hasn't decided to restore my body to its original condition, He has tenderly healed my soul into something stronger and more grace-shaped than it was before I even knew I needed healing. The healing I've experienced has been subtle and secret, but it's exactly the healing I needed most.

If it's true for me, could it be true for you too?

WHEN THERE'S NOTHING I CAN CONTROL ON THE OUTSIDE, I CAN ALWAYS GROW STRONGER INSIDE.

34

THE PORTRAIT

My stroke and the sixteen-hour, lifesaving surgery that followed caused catastrophic trauma to my brain. In fact, I was placed in a medically induced coma just to give my brain space to recover. I didn't snap out of it or wake up at any particular moment. Rather, the heavy fog of sedation lifted over months. It took just as long for me to begin to make sense of what had happened.

Needless to say, a near-vegetative state doesn't allow for much primping in the mirror or snapping the perfect selfie. (To be fair, my life before the stroke didn't have much of that either!) I knew something was different because of the new numbness in my face and my severe double vision, but reality would wallop me with full force when I finally looked in a mirror for the first time after my stroke. I saw a stranger.

The right side of my young face drooped like dough, and no amount of begging from my brain seemed to make the muscles budge. One corner of my mouth was turned down in a perma-frown, and my right eye crossed inward.

I didn't scream in horror or cry. I simply stared at the stone-cold evidence of my new reality, the visible proof of so much invisible loss. All I could manage to think was, *What now?*

Years later, a friend commissioned a portrait of me by an artist who specializes in painting people with disabilities in a dignifying way. I had made peace with my new face, but seeing it stretched across five feet of canvas felt like an unattainable feat of self-love. "Maybe a tasteful, locket-sized portrait would be preferable!" I offered. But after seeing the finished product, I was proven wrong.

The portrait features my face, turned slightly away, with my crooked smile and drooping eye on full display. My head is rendered in soft but hyperrealistic detail, while my shoulders fade away into a background of sweeping, abstracted clouds. If a person is allowed to make such bold assessments of her own likeness, I dare to say the piece is downright breathtaking.

I didn't cry when I saw my poststroke face in the mirror for the first time, but you better believe I ugly-sobbed when I saw this painting. I was moved to tears by its authenticity and dignity, its brokenness and beauty. My portrait told my story—a gorgeous balance of goodness and hardship that is rarely acknowledged, much less embraced, in real life.

We all will confront the reality of our post-disaster lives. We all will come face-to-face with the confirmation of our losses and they will beg us to answer the question, *What now?*

My friend, you don't have to be afraid of the answer. If you ask Him, God will grant you the grace to confront your new reality with both sober clarity and radical hope. He will give you eyes to see every bit of beauty in your busted-up-ness.

So, *what now* for me? Now, I'll keep staring back at my reflection—at my story— and accept the state of my situation day after day. And the longer I study the woman staring back at me and learn to appreciate the life she is living out, the more beauty I find. A beauty seen best through the blur of double vision. A beauty made deeper because it was birthed from unimaginable loss.

If it's true for me, could it be true for you too?

GOD CAN GRANT ME THE GRACE TO CONFRONT MY NEW
REALITY WITH BOTH SOBER CLARITY AND RADICAL HOPE.

35

BABY SHOES, NEVER WORN

When I became pregnant with John six years after my stroke, Jay and I were elated. That elation was quickly tempered by the sobering realization that we had not parented a newborn in almost seven years. (And since then, we'd aged what felt like seventy years!) We promptly began the baby boot camp of preparing our home and lives for this much-anticipated new addition.

At the time, we lived in a small California bungalow. (Like, tiny. Whatever you're imagining right now, shrink it by half, then take away a room, then dump in about a million LEGO blocks.) Despite the small-space living, we'd hung on to a lot of James's old baby clothes and toys. His first few years of life had been a blur of hospitals, rehab facilities, temporary living situations, storage units, and live-in caretakers. Practically, we had been too occupied with surviving to purge his closet. But I admit that we were nursing a tiny flicker of hope that his baby clothes might be put to use again one day.

Turns out, they would be. So as my belly grew rounder with John, we embarked on the catharsis of sorting through the tower of plastic tubs that held James's babyhood. Halfway through our organizing, Jay produced a tiny pair of saddle oxfords from the bottom of a bin. They were beige and white, almost as wide as they were long, with perfectly clean cotton laces.

For a moment, I didn't recognize the shoes. From the looks of them, they'd never been worn. Then I remembered. Right after James was born, the shoes had been given to him by one of his Southern grandmothers to wear with his fancy clothes. But fancy clothes and shoes had not made it onto our list of priorities when James was six months old and his mother was hooked up to life support in an intensive care unit.

As Jay and I looked at the little shoes in the palm of his hand, that famous six-word story popped into my mind: *For sale: baby shoes, never worn.*

I shuddered. If things had turned out just a little differently, those six words could have told our story. I suppose in some ways they did tell our story. But it wasn't the whole story. I acknowledged those little shoes represented an excruciating chapter, and we had grieved the losses of that time wholeheartedly. As I cradled the new life in my belly and instructed Jay to place the saddle oxfords in the keep pile, I decided that the shoes would now represent a chapter of redemption, a season of miraculously fulfilled hopes.

When we are deep in fresh experiences of suffering, we can delude ourselves into believing our stories have come to an end. Relics of an unexpected past can remind us how unknowable and uncontrollable the future will be. What do you see when you look ahead? A big blank space waiting to be filled with doom and dread? I think we've all been there. But we can reframe that emptiness as the pages on which God will write many more good/hard chapters. That empty expanse could be called *anxiety*. Or it could be called *hope*.

Those tiny shoes went unworn for a while, yes. Then they were worn for approximately three minutes by a miraculous (and strong-willed) little brother who couldn't stand to keep them on his feet. Nevertheless, the story wasn't over, and it still isn't over. Thank God He's not done writing any of our stories yet.

If it's true for me, could it be true for you too?

I CAN VIEW AN UNKNOWN FUTURE AS THE SPACE IN WHICH
GOD WILL WRITE MORE GOOD/HARD CHAPTERS OF MY STORY.

36

A MILESTONE
MISADVENTURE

I stared at the closed door in front of me and took a deep breath. The last thing I wanted to do was go through it. Since my stroke, I had developed a deep and irrational fear of public restrooms. They were one of the few spaces into which Jay couldn't always accompany me, and I had created an extensive catalog of elaborate daydreams in which I was attacked or kidnapped (and unable to defend myself or run away) inside a gas station bathroom. Before you judge me for developing a phobia of a one-in-a-million scenario, please remember that I've already survived a one-in-a-million scenario.

We were on a family road trip and I had gulped down a regrettable amount of sparkling water and coffee during the ride. I held it in as long as I could but eventually waved the white flag and asked that we pull over at the next gas station. Jay walked me inside and reassured me he'd be standing right outside the door the entire time I was in the bathroom.

I entered the room, keeping my back against the wall for support since my wheelchair could not navigate the tiny space—and because that's what people always did in the movies when entering a threatening situation. My permanent double vision prevented me from being able to clearly see which stalls were occupied, so I mustered every ounce of courage I could find and chose a stall to open at random. Adrenaline was coursing through my veins as I prepared myself for the knife-wielding murderer who would surely be waiting for me inside the stall.

From the hallway, Jay heard two bloodcurdling screams. Without hesitation, he burst into the women's bathroom to come to my rescue. Instead of finding me being held at gunpoint, he discovered that I was actually the perpetrator in the overcrowded restroom. In my state of high alert, I had opened the bathroom stall on an older woman whose only crime had been forgetting to latch the door before getting to her business. We both screamed and stared at each other in horror until we realized neither of us posed the slightest threat to the other. I apologized profusely and fumbled to close the door to the stall. Jay backed out of the room and tried to hide his hysterical laughter.

At some point in each of our lives, the world will prove that it is not a safe place for us. Our irrational fears will start to seem a little more rational. The threat of more suffering will lurk around every corner. If there are days you feel scared to step out of your own front door, you are not crazy. And you are certainly not alone.

It's tempting to convince ourselves that reentering an unsafe world in search of some bit of goodness or normalcy is not worth risking more pain, more humiliation, or more loss. Friend, I speak from experience. But much of the goodness of my second-chance life I've experienced came through the risks I've taken to find it. Could the risk be worth it for you? I'd say yes.

Over the past decade and a half, I have inched my way back into the world. The steps have been small, but the faith required has been enormous. My semisuccessful solo mission into a public bathroom proved to me that I could fumble my way back into the world. My bravery is clumsy and the adventures are almost always awkward, but I'm discovering a new kind of independence.

Sure, the world is not the safe place I once thought it was. But I am so much stronger than I ever imagined I could be. Here on the other side of suffering, I'm pretty convinced the world better watch out for me, because *here I come!*

If it's true for me, could it be true for you too?

THE WORLD MAY BE LESS SAFE THAN I ONCE THOUGHT, BUT I AM MUCH STRONGER THAN I EVER IMAGINED I COULD BE.

37

THE FRONT ROW

Over a decade ago, Jay and I were on the edge of our thirtieth birthdays and feeling the itch to celebrate with a fabulous trip. Or at least a trip as fabulous as a tight budget, young parenthood, and significant disabilities would allow! We hadn't traveled internationally since my stroke but felt brave enough to tackle a brief Italian getaway.

So many moments from our trip—like the insurance nightmare of an encounter between our rented Smart Car and a steep set of ancient cobblestone stairs—will stay with me forever. But the memory I treasure most is our morning at the Vatican. Jay's birthday happened to fall on Palm Sunday that year so, like any Southerners worth their salt, we got ourselves to a church. Running on "wheelchair time," we showed up a little late to the service in St. Peter's Square. We assumed we'd have to crane our necks from the back row to get a glimpse of the festivities. Instead, to our amazement and confusion, we were ushered by a series of nuns and security guards to the very front row of the enormous crowd. Beside us sat all the other attendees with disabilities.

Moments later, a procession of clergy walked through the crowd, holding large, beautiful palm fronds, with the pope himself bringing up the rear. He ascended the marble steps right in front of us. Seriously, I could have stretched my toes to touch the platform he was standing on. Still in shock over our front-row seats to this once-in-a-lifetime worship service, we sobbed through the choral performance, prayers, and papal address.

Although almost none of the message was delivered in English, few services have proven more memorable or meaningful to me. God changed me that day by giving me a new way to witness my own story of suffering. Because of my wheelchair, Jay and I were ushered to the very best seats in the square, not among dignitaries or famous guests but next to other people with disabilities and their families. In those sacred moments, God showed me that my weakness was the channel through which He would show His strength to the world.

Let's think extremely generously when we look for glory. It might not be in the pomp and perfection, where we expect to find it. When we take care to tune in to "the works of God" displayed all around us (John 9:3), it's like we're claiming a God-given front-row seat to our own glorious, hurting, but hopeful stories.

That morning at the Vatican gave me bright hope for a future filled with all kinds of grace moments, big and small. I'll probably never see the works of God being displayed within spitting distance of the pope again. That was pretty singular. But I know God is displaying His works all around me every day—even in the wounding, even in the losses, even in my very own disabled body that is giving my soul a miraculous second-chance life.

If it's true for me, could it be true for you too?

I'VE BEEN GIVEN A FRONT-ROW SEAT TO MY OWN
GLORIOUS, HURTING, BUT HOPEFUL STORY.

38

CHOSEN, NOT CURSED

During my fifteen years of living in a disabled body, hundreds of well-meaning people have leaned over my wheelchair, clutched both my hands, and told me, "I had the *exact same thing* happen to me! Can you believe it?" I usually couldn't believe it because, unlike me, they were traipsing through life with seemingly zero physical deficits. "Isn't God just *too* good?" they'd ask.

"He's been real good to *you*," I'd respond, if only inside my head.

Those accidental comparisons once stung me. Connections drawn with the intention of making me feel less alone actually threw the loneliness of my circumstances into striking relief. Sometimes I would just pretend they had spoken into my deaf ear so I didn't have to fake enthusiasm. (I highly recommend this tactic to anyone who can get away with it!) These interactions gave me the same feeling as being passed over for a game of dodgeball in a junior high gym class. Rejected rather than chosen. Forgotten instead of honored.

Thanks to the healing power of time—and a *whopping* investment in therapy—I feel at home in my unexpected story and disabled body. In fact, it rarely occurs to me to wish for any other reality. While I'll never understand God's role in human suffering, I hold a bone-deep belief that the story of my life was chosen by God for me with intention and care. With that conviction comes the freedom to feel genuine joy for someone else and their "happier" story. Now I can even celebrate with my friends who left the hospital unscathed and rejoice with those who seemed to bypass the deepest trenches of pain.

And I'm even more surprised by how my experience has grown my compassion and heartbreak for those people who may not be physically disabled on the outside but live with debilitating wounds of the mind or spirit. When you are so familiar with pain yourself, you are able to see the interior pain of everyone around you, no matter how okay they appear on the outside. But I'd be lying if I said I never longed for the physical freedoms some of my hurting friends still enjoy.

So when jealousy or dissatisfaction come calling, I remind myself not one of us was ever guaranteed a single day on this planet. I remember the reality of my miraculous second-chance life that has humbled and softened my spirit in ways a "perfect" story never could have. Almost every day of my poststroke life has been an imperfect but undeniable testament to the truth that God does not make mistakes. His intention for my life did not get lost in the shuffle or misassigned to another person's story in the cosmic assembly line. I was chosen. Not cursed. And I believe the same is true for you.

When I choose to embrace the life in front of me and release the life I imagined, I realize this good story is being written by a God who doesn't write any other kind of story. I am fully accepting the broken-down, miraculous nature of my life each day. This imperfect life is not a mistake. It was the one chosen just for me, and it's worth living well to the very end.

If it's true for me, could it be true for you too?

I AM CHOSEN, NOT CURSED.

39

LESSONS IN IMPROV

The hot stage lights beat down on me and blinded me from seeing the audience in the auditorium. My scene partner was coming to the end of his big monologue, and my line was next. I locked my focus onto the scene at hand and felt a surge of adrenaline. This was the biggest moment of my acting career thus far: the 1999 Georgia High School Association (GHSA) State One Act Play Championships.

With obsessively rehearsed timing, I began delivering my line. But midsentence, I felt a sickening *pop* around my waist, then a suspicious loosening. Without even glancing down, I knew the skirt of my costume had somehow malfunctioned and was, very conspicuously, making its way south. With enormous relief, I remembered I was wearing a petticoat. *Just go with it, Katherine!* I told myself as my skirt hit the stage floor. I recited my final line with all the conviction I could muster, kicked my skirt into the air, snatched it with my hand, then swung it over my shoulder as I exited stage left.

Backstage, I crumbled. I had blown the scene. Life simply could not go on after this career-ending faux pas. Eventually, I collected myself and joined the rest of my costars in the auditorium to watch the remainder of the competition and awards ceremony.

I wasn't even paying attention when the award for the Best Actress in the State of Georgia was presented. My friends had to tell me that *my name* had been called! It wasn't an Academy Award, but I accepted it with the same wide-eyed shock of every unsuspecting winner who just knew their name would never be called. Back in my seat, I looked over the judges' comments. Every single one noted how much they'd loved my comedic *choice* to lose the skirt.

Years later, a dear friend would point out to me that I was the ultimate "oh-well girl." When I told her that I didn't know whether to receive that as a compliment, she explained that she admired my willingness to improvise. No matter what life threw at me, I seemed to be able to throw my hands up, say "Oh well!" and pivot. Today I call this *emotional agility*.

As evidenced by my post-performance breakdown, I haven't always been able to roll with the punches. As silly as it sounds, winning that acting award when I was seventeen introduced me to a huge lesson: developing emotional agility could change how I handled hardship. I'd always been great at improvising onstage, but I would need to learn to improvise in *life*.

I had no idea how important that skill would be when my reality went off script. This time, it wouldn't be a costume malfunction but a major medical crisis. Of course, my response to having a stroke in my twenties wasn't a flippant "Oh well!" It looked more like years of fumbling through a scene that I really hated starring in.

Once I realized I wasn't returning to the original script anytime soon, I threw myself into the new one with as much enthusiasm and creativity as I could manage. Now I never miss a chance to publicly proclaim how much I love my life. I starve my fear of being dependent on others by asking for help when I need it. I actively replace the feelings of shame over my paralyzed face with a wild gratitude for my emancipation from beauty standards. This is what I mean by emotional agility. What might it look like in your version of an off-script life?

When I started acting like this unexpected turn of events had been the plan all along, my feelings about my circumstances changed. I'll keep embracing the role I've been given and imperfectly improvising my way through to the very end. And I sure hope I'm putting on a show worth watching.

If it's true for me, could it be true for you too?

DEVELOPING EMOTIONAL AGILITY CHANGES
HOW I HANDLE UNSCRIPTED HARDSHIP.

40

MY NEW VOICE

God overserved me when He was distributing the gift of gab. My mother never misses an opportunity to remind me that I was speaking in full sentences before my first birthday. And that once I started talking, I never stopped. I've always longed to be a part of the global conversation, and I've never hesitated to make my voice heard.

I did not give much thought to my actual voice—its tone and quality—until I lost it. On April 21, 2008, just before my hemorrhaging brain drowned out my consciousness, I uttered the last few words my "old voice" would ever speak. During the ensuing operation that would save my life, the neurosurgeon severed some intracranial nerves, which paralyzed the right side of my tongue, lips, and vocal cords. My musical, bright voice would exist only in recordings from that time on.

I wouldn't regain my ability to speak for months. I had a tracheostomy (an opening through the neck into the windpipe), so even when I began forming simple words with my mouth, I had to use my hand to cover the opening in order to produce any sound. That sound was a weak croak, not my voice. Eventually, my tracheostomy tube was removed and I relearned the subtle movements of my tongue, lips, and throat that had once happened without a thought. My poststroke voice sounded stretched and hoarse, less clear and lilting than it once was. I sounded like a stranger even to myself.

A couple of years after my stroke, I was due for a new cell phone. I made the big upgrade from my trusty BlackBerry to the much-buzzed-about iPhone (ah, the early 2010s!), and as I was getting all the settings sorted out, the iPhone prompted me to record a new voice mail greeting. Finger hovering over the Record button, I realized

I would be erasing the voice mail greeting I'd had for years before my stroke. My old "Hi, you've reached Katherine!" would be gone forever.

I had a new voice now and I dared to like it. Yes, it sounded different, but this voice was able to communicate truths my old voice never could have. This new version of me had experienced God's faithfulness and power in ways my old self had not. This new voice also had questions—lots of them—about suffering and God's goodness that my old voice never would have asked. Thankful for the ability to even speak at all and confident in the new voice I'd been given, I matter-of-factly recorded a new voice mail greeting.

I forgot to tell Jay about the update, so the first time he called me and got my voice mail greeting, he was taken aback. At first, the recording felt like cruel proof of all we'd lost. But with a little time, he was able to hear my new voice like I heard it—as the perfect medium for my second-chance story.

To an untrained ear, maybe your new voice doesn't sound any different from the old one. But if you listen closely, it is telling your story in a whole new way. Your new voice is richer now, layered with both authority and humility. It may sound unrecognizable, even to you. Even so, you can own it. Use it. Trust it. The world needs to hear "I'm still here" hope in the voice God has given you, and only you.

My new voice, in all its imperfection, now communicates with tens of thousands of people each year at speaking engagements, records audio versions of our books, prays over people who are in unfathomable pain, and stirs up dinner table conversations with my sons (who are as talkative as their mom). My new voice is narrating my new story. It's resounding and resonating in the places my old voice couldn't go.

If it's true for me, could it be true for you too?

GOD HAS GIVEN ME A NEW VOICE TO TELL MY NEW STORY.

41

MODELING AGAIN

We set off on our grand post-wedding adventure to Los Angeles with sights set on law school for Jay and a career in entertainment for me. After landing such coveted gigs as modeling a Tiki Room–themed muumuu in a Disneyland catalog or being hired as a stand-in for a popular actress when a shot required only the back of her head to be seen, I felt like I had *made it*. The five-year plan was really shaping up toward inevitable Oscar gold and being known by just my first name. And when baby James made his unexpected appearance, my career did not take a hiatus. I just booked jobs for the both of us!

Then came the stroke that paralyzed half my face and took away my ability to walk. That kind of put a crimp in my burgeoning career. Eventually, I came to terms with the fact I would never model again. I couldn't imagine how that part of my past could ever resurface, no matter how creative God got.

About four years after my stroke, I received a phone call from the head of marketing for the American Stroke Association. She had heard my story and thought I would be the perfect fit for their upcoming public awareness campaign educating America on the warning signs of a stroke.

Accepting the job was not an easy yes for me. The opportunity stirred up a lot of fear and embarrassment. It felt like another reminder of all that had changed in my life. But after a lot of prayers and encouragement from Jay, I accepted the job. Once I committed to embracing the situation, I had a blast filming the spot. And I really had a blast visiting the craft services table every fifteen minutes to take advantage of all the free treats!

Being the spokesperson for the American Stroke Association meant my little, crooked smile was plastered everywhere from Times Square to billboards in our own neighborhood in Atlanta. To this day, I still feel a tiny shock of surprise when my own larger-than-life face speeds past me on the side of a city bus.

A few years after the campaign aired, we heard it was one of the most effective public service announcements in the history of the Ad Council of America. I got to play a small part of bringing lifesaving education to millions of people about the second-leading cause of death in the world at the time.[4]

Realizing my most successful modeling gig (by *far*) happened *after* my stroke—with a paralyzed face, no less!—was a profound lesson in how God wrings out beauty from the driest places. I got the chance to model again not despite my imperfections but *because* of them. The outward signs of my brokenness helped save lives. That's as accurate a picture of the kingdom of God as I've ever seen.

Within our deepest hurts, insecurities, vulnerabilities, and shame, we have something more life-giving than our perfection could ever offer: an opportunity for grace.

As you can see, I have now arrived at the top. It's still about as glamorous as twirling in a Tiki Room muumuu but immeasurably more meaningful. This most unexpected mix of my commercial-model past and my stroke-survivor present taught me that God can use my deepest wounds to bring healing to the world.

If it's true for me, could it be true for you too?

GOD CAN USE MY DEEPEST WOUNDS TO
BRING HEALING TO THE WORLD.

42

HOPE IN THE FLESH

If you're like me, your spiritual life can feel pretty disconnected from your physical life. Spirituality often seems like it's on a plane of its own. In my youth, I left my curiosity about matters of the body to glossy fashion magazines or that random sorority sister who was always selling some magical, health-enhancing (pyramid scheme) protein shake. But after trauma affected my body in almost every way imaginable, my understanding of Jesus' time in a human body has changed completely.

Jesus' stay on earth in a flesh-and-blood body was intentional, not incidental. By all accounts, He lived among us in a body as unruly and ordinary as yours and mine. We can imagine how He plucked out a wiry gray hair or felt a bit self-conscious about that one weird toe. We know for certain that He showed immense compassion for those experiencing physical suffering. He paid attention to the hunger and sickness of the people around Him. Eventually, Jesus' own beaten body became the conduit of truest healing as He died for us on the cross. The early church even called themselves "the body of Christ."

The God-given goodness of our bodies is affirmed again and again in Scripture. But that affirmation can feel complex for those of us who are aging, who live with disabilities or chronic illnesses, who feel betrayed by bodies that don't function as they "should," who have been conditioned to regard our bodies as an enemy.

On a late April day, the body I had known for twenty-six years was replaced with a stranger's body. I would spend years learning new routes of navigating the world. I grappled with what it means to be "wonderfully made" (Psalm 139:14) with a brain defect that was knitted and knotted together when I was in my mother's womb. Even in the healing and adapting, I felt betrayed by my body. It felt like a barrier to the blessings God had for me.

I've come to notice God has a habit of blending the beautiful stuff and the broken stuff to create something far greater than the sum of its parts. I learned (and am still learning) my poststroke body is not a barrier to experiencing God's goodness. It's actually a part of God's pattern of using the most beaten-down among us to embody His resurrection power.

Second Corinthians 4:7 calls us all "jars of clay" filled with the treasure of God's good news. I love that whimsical word picture as much as the next jar, but am I the only one who feels like God made me a little too earthen and crumbly? *Maybe try using some rebar next time, Big Guy!*

Even in all their dysfunction, my tangled brain and eyes with double vision are helping me experience some of God until the day I can experience Him in full. This body is my one and only interface with reality, as busted up as it may be. This body carries me through my life. This body matters deeply to Jesus. So it should matter to me too.

When your body disappoints you, or even hurts you, you can rename it as a blessing instead of a burden. Your body is a flesh-and-blood example of Christ's perfect power playing out through imperfect means. Jesus has dignified your body, even if it feels broken. And that makes your body worthy of being called *good.*

I'm training myself to celebrate rather than just tolerate my broken brain and body because they didn't ruin my perfect life; they gave me the gift of a good/hard life. Because my body has suffered, my soul has flourished. Because my health and wellness failed me in every material way, my life embodies hope. Because I live in this fallible human body, I can know Jesus a little better.

If it's true for me, could it be true for you too?

GOD USES MY MOST BEATEN-DOWN PARTS TO
EMBODY HIS RESURRECTION POWER.

43

WHEELCHAIR-FREE

The first three years Jay and I lived in Los Angeles, I put a full one hundred thousand miles on our hand-me-down SUV. (I'm so sorry, planet Earth.) At the time, it never occurred to me just how limitlessly I was living. But in April 2008 I would drive for the last time. I would schlep James's car seat up the two flights of stairs to our law school apartment for the last time. I would be free, in one sense of the word, for the last time.

After I became disabled, I heard the language surrounding disability in a startling new way. The words that once described a distant *other* were suddenly being used to describe me. Genuinely well-meaning people would casually (and carelessly) use bizarre words like *crippled*, *victim*, and even *disfigured*.

The phrase that really lodged inside my head was *wheelchair-bound*. For a really long time, I bought into that language and let it tell me how to feel about my own life. The wheelchair, I believed, held me back from what I was entitled to do. It was a source of shame and hindrance. But don't we all have our own versions of "wheelchair-bound"? Unwanted singleness, limited finances, caregiving responsibilities, infertility, or unmet career aspirations. In one way or another, each of us feels bound by something.

Eventually, I got to know some people with disabilities who interacted with their own (literal and figurative) wheelchairs like assets rather than liabilities. These friends gave me new words for—and a new way of thinking about—my seat in life. My stroke happened and my ability to balance and walk was lost. Those are the facts. But here's what is also true: within my specific circumstances, my wheelchair doesn't confine or bind me. My wheelchair actually sets me free! It allows me to show up in the world, to move around safely, to travel through airports, to tag along with my kids to the park. I'm not wheelchair-bound. I am, in a sense, wheelchair-*free*.

The newfound freedoms did not stop with my wheelchair. Once I gave myself permission to think about my circumstances with hopeful imagination, I began to see the freedoms my stroke had offered me. And I truly believe your places of tightest constraint and limitation are offering you unexpected freedom too.

For instance, the possibility of "having it all" is simply not an option for me. While some people around me seem to balance family, career, health, travel, and a photoshoot-ready home with ease, I'm content with the freedom of knowing I can't even pretend to compete with other moms, with other public speakers, or with other adults in general. Heck, maybe even with most kids! I'll never be able to keep up with the Joneses, and that's okay because I'm not interested in their lives anyway. I'm focusing on my assignment and I'm not too worried about anyone else's.

I've also been set free from the jangle of messages competing to tell me the story of my beauty. As I've adjusted to life with a partially paralyzed face, I've had no other choice but to release the ludicrous cultural beauty standards I had been given and replace them with something truer and deeper. Now I'm free to call myself beautiful because I have survived and been refined by suffering, not because I finally got my hair and makeup just right.

Above all, I have been set free to radically love my life even if I'm not "supposed" to love it. Even if no one else envies the reality I've been handed. My stroke gave me the freedom to *decide* that I want my life because it's the life I have. I can say with gut-deep honesty that I wouldn't change it if I could. And to me, that sounds a lot like true freedom.

If it's true for me, could it be true for you too?

TRUE FREEDOM IS DECIDING TO WANT THE LIFE I
HAVE BECAUSE IT'S THE LIFE I WAS GIVEN.

44

REMEMBERING THE
RIGHT STORY

Recently, Jay and I were discussing what an acutely difficult year 2020 had been for a close friend of ours. With lots of guilt, we both admitted that 2020 had been fine for us. We'd been spared so much of the loss and instability wreaked by that year. The option of busyness was taken from us, so we were able to turn inward toward each other and our boys. We were given glorious permission to go into full hermit mode and probably still haven't fully recovered our pre-pandemic social graces. But that's an issue to unpack another day!

As the conversation continued, we began retracing the reality of the 2020 we had actually lived. We chuckled as we started rattling off all the intensely, heinously hard parts of that year: Maintaining a nonprofit and full-time staff through global financial insecurity. Wrangling two hyperactive sons during months of virtual learning. Watching my dad contend with a rare and aggressive cancer. Canceling dozens of speaking events and sweating a little over the lost income. Shifting our beloved Hope Heals Camp to a virtual format. Navigating some intense marital conflict. And, for the grand finale, ending 2020 with a serious fall that required major surgery on my blown-out ACL, MCL, and meniscus.

Yeah, our 2020 had in fact been pretty wild and rough too.

This walk down a rocky memory lane is a microcosm of the lesson we've been learning every day since my stroke: the facts of what happened to us matter far less than the way we remember what happened to us. Remembering well allows us to re-narrate our old stories and, in so doing, anticipate a more hope-filled future.

I've lived an exceptionally hard story, and maybe you have too. But for me, it would be irresponsible and untruthful to just call my story a bad one. My life is bearable because I've decided to identify the truest story—the good, the bad, and the ugly—and tell it in the most beautiful way I can. Telling my redefined story isn't about denying the hard facts of my past. It's about unearthing all the treasure I can find in the darkest places of my life.

What about your story? We're all historians narrating the story *of* us *to* us, but the amazing thing is we have the option to redefine the hard parts of our stories. When we cling to the tragic details and most depressing plotlines of our lives, our brains expect tragedy and depression in the pages to come. But when we choose to narrate our stories with complex beauty, nuanced grace, and constant gratitude, our brains can begin to anticipate goodness ahead. Re-narrating doesn't erase the bad stuff, but it does reveal our uniquely human capacity to find hope in every chapter. What can you remember well today? What is the truest version of the story of your life?

For me, responsible remembrance has become a bit of past-changing magic that gives me the grace of distance. It opens up space for gratitude and perspective to redefine my past, present, and future. The past is a fact, but the way I tell my story is a choice.

If it's true for me, could it be true for you too?

WHEN I CHOOSE TO TELL THE TRUE STORY OF MY PAST,
I CAN ANTICIPATE GOODNESS IN THE FUTURE.

I 'm still not exactly sure how I broke my leg.

By summer 2012, I had clocked innumerable hours relearning to walk in the four years that had passed since my stroke. While I still relied on a wheelchair for trips of any significant distance, I had begun to take a little pride in my new party trick of stringing a few steps together all on my own. My updated gait was wobbly and wonky, but in the technical sense of the word, I was walking again!

Jay, James, and I were in the thick of our annual Deep-Fried Southern Tour and had landed at my parents' home in Georgia for a few days. James had been playing in a room down the hall from me, and I wanted to pop my head in to check on him. En route to my desired destination, I somehow tripped (despite the fact that the floor was flat) and lost my balance (despite the fact that I was walking with one hand on a cane and the other against a wall). My upper body and lower body twisted in opposite directions as I fell through the air. A sickening, splintering sensation shot up my right leg. Then I hit the floor.

Within minutes, a team of medics hoisted me onto a stretcher and out of the house, and I went into surgery the next morning. My surgeon determined the only way to repair the spiralized shattering of my tibia and fibula was to insert a metal rod—a horrifying eighteen inches long!—into my leg. The break was pretty devastating physically, of course. But my spirit took the biggest beating. This half-second fall set me back literal years in regaining my ability to walk.

We rearranged our remaining summer plans, and I spent the next few weeks laid up in a rented hospital bed in my parents' living room. I felt like frailty personified. The new addition of the metal rod caused me a ton of pain as my leg slowly healed, but at least it earned me a pretty great nickname from my friends and family: the "Steel Magnolia."

Little did I know that the metal rod, which had become a permanent part of me, would prevent me from shattering my leg again eight years later. In 2020, the awkward spill off my adaptive bike caused terrible damage to my knee and ligaments, but my tibia, which should have splintered again, sustained only a thin fracture. My leg withstood an incredibly intense impact without breaking, and I have that darn metal rod to thank. The leg that had been broken and remade was stronger *because* of the breaking, not despite it.

The notion that our pain can be used for good is hard to accept. In fact, it can feel downright sadistic sometimes. But so many big and small stories in my life continue to prove to me that suffering can be an opportunity to cultivate strength in the places I thought were weak.

I'm learning that our brokenness doesn't necessarily disqualify us from wholeness. Instead, brokenness can lead to a kind of healing that makes us so much more whole than we ever were before the breaking. If you join God in the hard work of healing, your scars become glorious badges of honor. They remind you that you suffered. But you also survived. And you're so much stronger for it.

My leg is reinforced with steel, and so is my spirit. I don't have to be so afraid of the spills and scrapes and sadnesses headed my way. Will they hurt? Of course they will. But I know I can be battered and bruised without fully breaking. I know the pain of my past—marked by scars and reinforced with steel—can be the very things that prevent me from breaking again. God has used my suffering to reinforce my soul.

If it's true for me, could it be true for you too?

SUFFERING IS AN OPPORTUNITY TO CULTIVATE STRENGTH
IN THE PLACES I ONCE THOUGHT WERE WEAK.

46

DREAMING NEW DREAMS

I 've always known I wanted to tell God's story from a public platform. Beyond even wanting to, I was certain I was meant to. As a child, I would line up my dolls against my bedroom wall and unload impassioned sermons on the glassy-eyed audience. (Wait . . . was I weird?) Eventually, I formulated a perfectly sensible plan to break into the entertainment industry, despite the slight complication that I was a wholesome Southern belle with uncompromising morals. It made sense at the time!

Precisely when I was gaining a small bit of traction in my modeling and acting career, my stroke extinguished my rising star and threw my well-laid plans into disarray.

In the early days of my recovery, I bristled at being called the "miracle girl" in the wheelchair. An uncharacteristic, visceral anger bubbled up in my gut every time someone gushed about the goodness of God's plan for me. My uncooperative limbs and drooping face and distorted voice appeared to be the exact opposite of a miracle. How would all this help me earn that Oscar I'd dreamed about since childhood? I already knew exactly how I'd humbly point upward and thank God as I accepted the award through graceful tears!

Not one bit of my situation seemed to fit into my plan, which I had accidentally mistaken as God's plan. Surely this wasn't the life I had been promised or the platform I'd been assigned. It certainly wasn't the fulfillment of any dream I'd ever had. Or nightmare, for that matter.

Our dreams for the future can anchor us in purpose and inspire us to make progress. Or they can sentence us to a lifetime of disappointment. Why are they so darn hard to let go of? I think it might be because letting go of a dream also means letting go of the version of yourself that dreamed the dream. And the version of yourself that was going to see that dream fulfilled. Burying a dream means burying the person you wanted to be. When our dreams are officially pronounced dead, our grief can block our vision of any new possibilities or new identities ahead of us.

As I settled into my new normal, I began sharing my story at small speaking engagements where I intersected with other "miracle" men and women with literal and invisible wheelchairs of their own. I realized my platform wasn't collateral damage of my stroke. Rather, my stroke had led me to these very people—my people!—and my pain had given me a platform to share all I was learning. God had allowed me to survive, to be a living embodiment of His hope in the world. He'd given me a new dream and a better plan. But it was up to me to recognize it.

Did disability or lifelong dependence or chronic pain make it onto my vision board for my life? You bet your Georgia peach they did not! But neither did my Hope Heals Camp community, a speaking career, or writing books. Not to mention the indescribable kinship I formed with Jesus because of my suffering. My wildest plans could not have contained the treasures I've found in the dark parts of my story.

Friend, so many of your dreams are good. They are worth cherishing, which means they are worth mourning too. But you can believe me when I say your best-laid plans pale in comparison to your divine purpose. So when old dreams die, you can move forward knowing that some of the very things that wrecked your dreams are actually clearing your path to a God-designed future.

When we draw hard lines of expectation around God's cooperation in our well-laid plans, our divine imaginations atrophy. This poststroke life has given me permission to dream new dreams within the boundaries set before me. And in so doing, I've experienced heights and depths and expanses that my old plans never could have contained.

If it's true for me, could it be true for you too?

I HAVE PERMISSION TO DREAM NEW DREAMS
WITHIN THE NEW BOUNDARIES OF MY LIFE.

47

DON'T WAIT TO CELEBRATE

You have not lived until you've eaten a Jay Wolf frittata. I will die on this hill. Since we first married, my dear husband has been able to access some magical alchemy that turns a bunch of forgotten ingredients from the far reaches of the refrigerator into the fluffiest, most flavorful eggy deliciousness. Sometimes Jay whips up a frittata on a run-of-the-mill Saturday morning. But usually, we save this family favorite for hosting guests on particularly special occasions. You know, like filing for bankruptcy or divorce, or losing a job or a loved one. (Hey, I didn't say *good* occasions. Just uniquely special ones.)

In the Wolf household we call these sacred shared meals our "brokenness brunches." I was inspired by my friend Sarah, who threw a party—"A tribulation celebration"—after her father was diagnosed with cancer. Her family gathered for good food, laughter, and, most of all, tears. They were not celebrating the cancer diagnosis. In fact, they were mourning it. But they were choosing to recognize the comforting reality that their dad was not facing his season of suffering all alone. Together, they were praising God in the process of their wounding. They decided, then and there, that their joy would not be determined by an outcome.

I rebranded Sarah's tribulation celebration into a brokenness brunch, despite Jay's heavy eye-rolling at my unabashed love of alliteration. For my first event, I selected some specific friends who were navigating particularly difficult situations. From financial fallout to kids with disabilities to mothers with mental illness, our little party thoroughly covered the spectrum of suffering. Sounds like a photo-worthy, hashtag-able brunch moment, doesn't it?

As we sat around the table at that first brokenness brunch, each of us was able to look someone in the eye who was surviving pain we couldn't imagine feeling. Instead of a pity party, this gathering invited each of us into a posture of perspective and then praise. We discovered there was deep healing to be found when we celebrated in the midst of our suffering, rather than waiting on desired outcomes. Even in the loss and unmet expectations, God had given us Himself. And He'd given us each other. So why wouldn't we celebrate that day?

We've expanded our brokenness brunches into a habit of unconventional celebrations. Every year, for instance, we celebrate the anniversary of the day *after* my stroke. We call it Katherine Lived Day. The date is marked by miracles, of course, but it still remains one of the hardest days of our lives. It's the source of so many yet-to-be-healed hurts. While I celebrate the surprise of getting a second chance at life, I don't celebrate from a place of completion or closure. Life is still in process and my health is still in a maddening state of instability. Even so, I'm fighting to celebrate with other co-sufferers in the messy, mysterious middle.

You're in some kind of middle of your own today, and teeth-gritted getting-through may feel like your only option. I'm sending this hand-addressed invitation from my heart to yours: don't wait to celebrate an outcome. Instead, celebrate the outworking of Divine Love in all its forms, right in the midst of your suffering. If the frittatas and fine china aren't quite your style, find some way—any way!—to commemorate God's provision and presence today.

The longer I live, the more the line blurs between the party and the pulpit. For me, celebration has become a form of worship, a joyful rebellion against fear and despair. (Leave it to me to make brunch sacred!) These days, I don't wait to celebrate desired outcomes or happy endings. I'm praising God for His provision, power, and presence in the process.

If it's true for me, could it be true for you too?

I DON'T HAVE TO WAIT TO CELEBRATE AN OUTCOME.
INSTEAD, I CAN CELEBRATE GOD'S PRESENCE AND
PROVISION IN THE MIDST OF MY SUFFERING.

48

MESS INTO MINISTRY

My husband has textbook-perfect taste. No matter the place we may call home at any given time, he has made it a haven of beauty, peace, and healing. My nightstand is never without a small vase of fresh flowers, the pillows on the couch are always neatly karate-chopped into submission, and a well-placed tchotchke can be found in every hidden nook.

But those tchotchkes didn't materialize out of thin air. They were collected by the dozens—along with antique furniture and artwork and family photographs and books and sentimental letters. Our countertops may be free of clutter, but our garage most certainly is not.

After I progressed from my brain rehab facility in the early days of my recovery, we moved into a teeny yellow craftsman bungalow that would have been the perfect size for about three of James's action figures to live in. Before long, the little house was filled to the brim with beautiful thrifted finds, as well as a mountain of mementos—from sorority T-shirts to old hospital bracelets—from our past lives and my recent near-death experience.

In 2013, once we had some speaking experience under our belts and had gained a modest online following, we officially formed Hope Heals. In December of that year, we received a very official-looking government letter certifying Hope Heals as a 501(c)(3). Having a single page of business documentation obviously meant we needed a full-blown home office, so we decided to convert a room of our house into a small workspace. This is when Jay's inner minimalist made its rare appearance. A purge was going down, and not a knickknack or keepsake (or any one of James's finger paintings) was safe.

During the purge, Jay tackled our small two-drawer filing cabinet since, of course, our prized nonprofit document needed a safe place to be stored. As he rifled through the overstuffed folders, he realized he was looking at hospital and insurance records that were long obsolete and no longer had a relevant place in our lives, even though they had taken up our whole universe at one point. Staring at the stack, Jay was transported to the moment a longtime prayer supporter had told us, "I originally thought I was just praying for a girl to survive a stroke. But what we were really praying for was the creation of a ministry."

With great satisfaction, Jay swapped the thick stacks of medical paperwork in that filing cabinet with the certification letter for a ministry that exists only because, for a little while, we were completely miserable. The business of surviving was officially behind us, and the important work of healing was at hand.

The piles of spiritual junk stored up in my soul tower over any literal junk stored in my house. If I take the time to sort through the overstuffed filing cabinets of my heart and mind, I realize I'm hanging on to old narratives and beliefs and dreams that no longer have a place in my life. They may be even less useful than the faded sorority shirts!

What's taking up precious space in your soul today? Maybe it's an experience of rejection. An identity of failure. A loss you can't move past. Could I convince you to believe that God is waiting to replace it with something immeasurably more valuable?

Since our home office makeover, we've accumulated many more stacks of regrettably relevant medical and insurance files because my health problems continue to intensify. But Jay keeps making our spaces beautiful. And God continues delighting and surprising us with the creative ways He is repurposing the past to bring beauty and goodness into the world. He has made my mess into a message and given me a ministry from my misery. I'm trusting Him to clear the clutter.

If it's true for me, could it be true for you too?

GOD WILL MAKE A MESSAGE OUT OF MY MESS.

49

VIEW FROM THE MIDDLE

Have a good time!" I shouted to my boys as they retreated from me. "I'll be waiting for you when you get back!"

I wasn't seeing them away to school or over to a friend's house. Of all things, I was sending them off to hike a volcano. And I had come to terms with the fact that I would not be joining them on the adventure.

Nearly twenty years ago, Jay and I honeymooned in Hawaii and made the three-mile round-trip hike up Waikiki's famous Diamond Head volcano with total ease. Well, maybe not total ease. The single piece of photographic evidence undeniably shows we'd both worked up quite a glisten beneath our finest early 2000s athleisure.

Recently, we returned to Hawaii to speak at a medical conference with wildly different abilities than our twenty-two-year-old selves. And, this time, with a couple of sons in tow! Powerless against the allure of a grand symbolic gesture, we decided we simply had to try to climb up Diamond Head again. We were itching to prove just how good God is. And, ahem, just how tough we still were. Grit, after all, is the tenth fruit of the spirit in my translation of the New Testament.

I started the hike on a paved path in my wheelchair. As the terrain got rougher, I left the chair and began walking while holding Jay's steady arm on the one-way trail. Each step felt a little more tenuous, and by the time we had made it halfway up, the rocky path had proven too much for me to negotiate. I desperately wanted to get to the top again. But even more, I wanted *not* to go to Waikiki General with a broken leg!

Jay and the boys were willing to carry me all the way up. They even began designing an impressively engineered cradle formed solely from forearms! In the end, I knew I was safer sitting on a bench at a nearby viewpoint. From the safety of my seat, I watched my three guys wind up the trail until they were the size of little ants.

In the privacy of my heart and in the solitude of my waiting, I felt like a failure. After all the life-and-death challenges I'd overcome, I should be able to hike a little mountain, for goodness' sake! In that moment, I caught myself attempting to do something you've probably tried to do too: Prove God to be powerful. Or good. Or faithful. Or trustworthy. Or whatever adjective you feel responsible for corroborating on His behalf.

Friend, God doesn't need our help proving that He is in control. He doesn't need our feats of strength or even our well-meaning grit to back up the fact that He's making all things new. We can join Him in the restoration work, but you and I will never be the ones to make the miracles happen. So take a deep breath. You can officially release the responsibility.

We've all longed to return to our glory days of long-gone adventures, to prove God's healing hand is at work in our lives. And sometimes that longing is fulfilled and the evidence is undeniable. But more often, we will not make it back to the mountaintops. Restoration won't always take the route we hoped it would.

As I enjoyed the island breeze during that rare hour of solitude on the side of a volcano, I realized I didn't have to make it to the top of every mountain. Being alive to attempt the climb was proof enough of God's goodness to me.

Eventually, the boys descended and proudly swiped me through about a thousand sweaty, sunsetty selfies from the top of Diamond Head. And you know what? Looking at the photos, I felt as exhilarated as if I'd summited Everest myself. In the years following my stroke, a trip to Hawaii would have seemed daunting. The hike up even half of Diamond Head, impossible. And doing it all with the addition of a poststroke son? Unfathomable.

My second-chance life hadn't brought me to the summit this time, but it had brought me back to the trailhead. And it had allowed my boys to experience the wonders of the view from the top. With gratitude for the path in front of me and perspective on how far I'd come, I'd decided to let God prove Himself with whatever evidence He wanted.

If it's true for me, could it be true for you too?

I AM NOT RESPONSIBLE FOR PROVING GOD'S REDEMPTIVE WORK IN MY LIFE. BUT I CAN JOIN IN ON IT.

50
STONES OF HELP

For years, an entire portion of our bedroom wall was dedicated to a floor-to-ceiling grid of tacked-up Polaroid pictures. The photos looked really great, but more importantly, they served a vital function in my life. They were the last thing Jay and I saw as we went to sleep and the first thing our eyes landed on each morning. The pictures told us the visual story of our lives. They were reminders of the best days and the worst days and all the forgettable days in between.

Once we moved into our new home in Atlanta, we were unwilling to sacrifice the gloriously fresh drywall to the million little holes our photo grid would require. So we piled the pictures into a big ceramic bowl and placed it on our coffee table, which happens to be the center of our family life and social life. The photos continue to tell us the story of our lives, and now we're inviting our loved ones to see the story with us.

There's a story in the Old Testament about the Israelites winning a particularly important battle with the help of God's miraculous intervention. Humans are forgetful, and the Israelites seemed to know this, so they set up a huge stone on the site of their victory to remind them—and the generations to come—of God's faithfulness. They called that stone an Ebenezer, which translates to "stone of help." Inspired by this story, Jay and I have made an effort to surround ourselves with seeable, touchable, experienceable Ebenezers of the goodness of God in our lives.

There's the overflowing bowl of Polaroids on our coffee table. There are the thick-framed black glasses I wore in neuro rehab, which Jay had mounted on pale-blue velvet and framed in a shadow box. There's the life-size abstract painting of Lazarus hung on our office wall. There's the bookshelf lined with *kintsugi* vases, which are beautiful *because* they've been broken and pieced back together. There's the healed-up trach scar above my collarbone.

And then, of course, there's each and every day of my second-chance life, the most potent reminder of God's miraculous intervention when I needed saving most desperately.

While my home is filled with Ebenezers, it's also littered with dirty dishes, an overflowing clothes hamper, the donation pile by the back door that still hasn't made it to Goodwill after literal years, and the general garbage found in any space shared with boys. And while my life itself is filled with reminders of God's faithfulness, it's also filled with the clutter of lost dreams and unmet expectations and the many valid reasons to fear the future.

Recognizing this messy reality is exactly how I remember that gratitude isn't just for holidays or the rare times I've got it all together. Every day, my imperfect Ebenezers invite me into a rhythm of remembrance. They ground me in grace. They remind me that God will show up again because He showed up already.

We can be so forgetful when it comes to remembering what God has done. In fact, we can convince ourselves that He's never come through, which means He won't come through the next time we need help. But that simply isn't true. Look around, friend. There is evidence of God's showing up everywhere you look. What "stones of help" could you gather for yourself to remind you of the places He's shown up?

I'm still on the lookout for Ebenezers of God's faithfulness myself. I've learned they are everywhere if I choose to look for them. I'm binding them to my heart to reinforce the good story being written between the lines of my life. I'm remembering that God helped me once, and He will help me again.

If it's true for me, could it be true for you too?

PHYSICAL EBENEZERS OF GOD'S FAITHFULNESS REMIND ME THAT GOD WILL SHOW UP AGAIN BECAUSE HE SHOWED UP ALREADY.

51

A MIRACLE ERRAND

I posted up on our tiny front porch, checking my phone notifications and eagerly glancing up at the road every time I heard a car pass. I felt jittery with excitement and nerves, something akin to stage fright. I was about to accomplish something I had not done since before my stroke. Drumroll, please.

I was going grocery shopping. *Alone.*

For you, a solo grocery trip may sound like a throwaway hour of the day, or even a chore. But to me, eight years poststroke at that point, it was a watershed moment.

I ordered a car from a ride-sharing app and was whisked away to Trader Joe's, my happiest place, by the marvel of modern technology. Once inside, I grabbed a cart to assist me in my wobbly loop around the grocery aisles. I fully intended on tossing in every last item that caught my fancy. Money was no object on such a monumental day. Besides, I had coupons!

Several times throughout my shopping trip, I paused in awe of this little independence—which felt like a *big* grace—that I had regained. Trader Joe's is a place of wonder under any circumstance, but that day it felt downright miraculous. In my story, big and small disappointments constantly threaten to obscure the grace and goodness tucked into my ordinary days. But seeing my life with gratitude helps me notice the wonder of it all spilling from the places I might have overlooked otherwise.

As soon as I reevaluated my standards for what deserves awe and gratitude, my world began overflowing with reasons for awe and gratitude. Errands become adventures and chores become treasures. Sure, I could have chosen to feel ashamed of the fact that I couldn't drive myself to the store. Or bitter over the reality that I couldn't pull off a grocery trip like this regularly. But I found a more useful response.

It may sound like I'm settling for less here, but I don't think I am. Settling for less would mean greedily reserving my wonder for the rare experiences and the few-and-far-between *wow* moments. What a sad way to live! Gently, I want to ask you how you might be withholding the gratitude and awe you could feel within your circumstances. What places in your life might be worth your wide-eyed wonder if only you decided to give them a closer look with more hopeful standards?

I commemorated that monumental pilgrimage to Trader Joe's by asking a kind (but understandably confused) stranger to take my photo in front of the checkout line. I instinctively grabbed a baguette from a nearby display for some reason, like a glutenous trophy. I was beaming with joy and gratitude.

Yes, the ride-share car smelled weird and the checkout line was insane and I had misread some of my coupons and there was nowhere to park when Jay came to fetch me at the end of the shopping trip. But as I pushed the cart out into the afternoon breeze, my whole body tingled with exhilaration. Who knew a trip to the grocery story could be such an unexpected gift? All I needed was a new standard that opened me up to seeing the world in a more generous way.

Shifting our baseline for goodness can feel like we are settling for scraps. Or it can free us to receive every last drop of the abundance we've been given, rather than pining for what we think we deserve. There's wonder tucked into my life today, waiting for me to notice it. And when I do, I want to remember it. Baguette photo optional.

If it's true for me, could it be true for you too?

SEEING MY LIFE WITH GRATITUDE HELPS ME NOTICE THE WONDER SPILLING FROM PLACES I COULD EASILY OVERLOOK.

52

THE LIFE-CHANGING LAUGH

T he stand-up comedian delivered the punch line of a semi-risky joke. For a millisecond, the room was suspended in that *Will it land?* tension that I knew all too well as a public speaker myself. We had never hired a stand-up comedian to perform at Hope Heals Camp before, and while this guy seemed great and all, I found my insides squirming in that instant between the joke and the audience's response. From the front row, I scanned the crowd with the anxiety of any self-respecting host and took in all the men and women in wheelchairs, all the parents enjoying a few hours of free childcare, all the souls living stories they'd never expected to live.

My worries dissolved in the enormous swell of laughter from the crowd, many of whom were literally slapping their knees. One holler rose above the rest and, as the general laughter tapered off, this high-pitched chuckle continued in full force. Which then made the crowd's laughter start up again. Even the comedian, uncontrollably tickled, couldn't manage to collect himself enough to resume the set. Every last one of us was laughing to the point of tears, and the waves of whoops just kept rolling in.

I quickly identified the source of the contagious laughter as my friend David, who had been joining us at Hope Heals Camp since our very first summer. As a young adult, David had contracted an infection that caused life-altering swelling and injury to his brain. His speech, mobility, and motor skills were significantly changed, and now he lives with his parents, who serve as his full-time caregivers. Although he communicates very differently than most people, David is hilarious, extroverted, and energetic. This giggling episode could not have been more fitting for him. The set eventually ended, and most of us were still breathless from the laughter.

The next morning our adult campers gathered for a time of worship and teaching in the same beautiful chapel in the woods where the comedian had performed the night before. As our musical guests led the group in an opening song, I scanned the crowd once again to make sure everyone seemed to be comfortable. My eyes caught on two upraised arms. Two arms that belonged to David, who was seated in his wheelchair at one of the front tables. David couldn't sing the lyrics at the same pace as the musicians, but he was fully and earnestly engaged in meeting God in that moment. His worship that morning was as full-bodied as his laughter had been the night before.

David taught me that laughter and worship aren't so different. In fact, they are simply two of the shapes that hope takes. Both laughter and worship are most powerful when offered from full brokenness of body or of circumstance. Sure, it's great to celebrate and praise God when life is good. But whooping with laughter when you can hardly speak or raising your hands in worship from the seat of a wheelchair . . . now that's evidence of a soul who has found transcending security and joy in Divine Love.

Suffering can harden us to the good things left in life, or it can open us up to receive them with abandon. We can recognize that not everything is perfect (or that nothing at all is perfect!) and continue to be grateful for what is deeply, unquestionably good. Even after the worst thing happens, we have unconditional permission to laugh to the point of tears and praise God with outstretched hands.

If it's true for me (and David), could it be true for you too?

SUFFERING CAN HARDEN ME TO THE GOOD THINGS LEFT IN MY LIFE, OR IT CAN OPEN ME UP TO RECEIVE THEM WITH ABANDON.

53

THE GIFT OF BAD TIMING

We've all experienced moments so satisfyingly synced with our hopes or needs that we can't help but credit divine oversight for the perfect timing. On the flip side, you and I have lived moments of (almost) laughably bad timing. So bad, it seems there had to be a degree of intentionality involved. A cosmic punch line perfectly delivered.

I am alive today because of a thousand miraculously timed moments and right-time-right-place provisions. But I've also had my share of ill-timed mishaps. In February of 2020, literally days before COVID-19 shut down the world, Jay and I released our second book, *Suffer Strong*. Over a decade in the making, *Suffer Strong* recounted the hard-won lessons learned from my second-chance life. It was forged with our blood, sweat, and tears. A true labor of love.

We humbly hoped all this effort would earn us a modest top-ten spot on the *New York Times* Best Sellers List at the very least! Instead, the world was plunged into a pandemic just days after the release of the book, and our much-anticipated launch was lost in the apocalyptic shuffle of 2020.

We had invested so much care into this book with the sincere desire of offering an ounce of comfort to hurting people. But our preparations could not outpace a pandemic, which was appropriately called an "act of God" according to all our voided speaking contracts that year. Neither could our best-laid plans overpower God's intended timeline for our message of suffering strong.

Candidly, we grappled with our disappointed hopes for *Suffer Strong* in an intense way. I know, I know. I could almost gag at how unrelatable this all sounds. Poor me. My book didn't sell a million copies. NBC's *TODAY* show never called for that interview. *TIME* must have gone a different direction with that cover feature. Get a grip, Katherine!

But haven't we all had our own stomach-dropping moment of perfectly bad timing? The one that seems to confirm our efforts were wasted. Our vulnerability, valueless. You don't need a discouraging book launch to relate to the feeling that God seemed to miss the divine appointment you had written on your calendar in ink. And if someone asks you to believe that it's for the best, it's hard to see how. But it sure is easy to roll your eyes.

Humor me here. What if God could actually still move through the "bad" timing? What if we replaced our belief in bad timing with trust in a really good God?

Today, with the grace of distance, we appreciate the poetic irony that our book about unmet expectations did not, in fact, meet our expectations. But the book we wrote did end up ministering to our own hearts. We can see that *Suffer Strong* actually showed up in the world exactly when it should have. It's almost as if God planned it that way, huh?

In early 2020—and far beyond—the world desperately needed a guide for suffering well. The book has quietly and steadily found its way into the hands of the people who need it most. Including Jay and me. We have been honored to act as conduits of and testaments to God's redemptive power, even if it hasn't looked the way we imagined. Which is pretty on-brand for us!

I'm going to keep showing up to this good/hard life and offering what I have. And in all the effort of showing up, I can leave the timing to the One who sets a perfect, on-purpose pace.

If it's true for me, could it be true for you too?

**I CAN REPLACE MY BELIEF IN BAD TIMING
WITH TRUST IN A REALLY GOOD GOD.**

54

CONVERSATIONS
WITH JOHN

What happened to you, Mom?" My son John presented the question without an ounce of self-consciousness or unkindness. Only pure curiosity. He is as bright as a child can be. I count conversations with him as one of the primary privileges of my life, so he has a standing invitation to ask me anything.

Unlike our firstborn, James, John has only ever known and been mothered by a disabled mom. He has always felt totally at ease with the presence of my wheelchair, my distorted voice, and my crooked smile. But when he was about five years old, he began noticing his mom was a little different from the other moms in the carpool pickup line or at Sunday morning church.

I figured an in-depth discussion on the intricacies of an arteriovenous malformation might tax his attention span, so I opted for the simple version. "Well, John, for most of my life, I was able to do all the things you see other grown-ups doing. But then my brain got really sick one day. All of a sudden, I looked a little different and I wasn't able to do everything I could do before," I explained as best I could.

John fixed his wide brown eyes on my half-paralyzed face as he considered this new information. He then replied, "I guess God fixed you, just not all the way. You are a little broken, but you're still working pretty good!"

Satisfied with his conclusions on the matter, John didn't bring up my disabilities again for years. But recently, a slightly more mature John asked whether the stroke had affected my mind or personality. Essentially, he wanted to know if I was the same person I'd been before the day that changed everything. I took time choosing my words because I wanted to steward this lesson on suffering with enormous care.

"The stroke didn't change my personality or my mind. I didn't lose any of my ability to think or express myself. But, John, the experience of suffering *did* change me. It transformed my mind and my personality in all kinds of ways. And actually, I am better because of it."

No one escapes suffering unscathed. It changes us forever. But we get to decide how it's going to change us. Dear one, an experience of suffering could devastate your fragile spirit just as severely as a stroke devastated my fragile body. It could leave you weak, bitter, and afraid. But that very same experience of suffering could also grind and polish you into something more beautiful, resilient, and complex than you ever were before. To borrow John's words, suffering may leave us a little broken, but we can still work pretty good.

The difference maker between devastation and transformation is the presence of hope. When we choose to hope that good things could come from our worst days, we change for the better. And when we choose to believe Divine Love remains with us, even when there's no redemption in sight, we change for the better.

One day soon I'll be able to tell John all I've learned from my journeys into darkness. But for now, I'll tell him that suffering is not the end. Not for him, and not for me. If I can keep waiting well during my deepest pains, my perseverance produces character, and my character produces hope. And the whole horrible, holy process produces change worth wanting.

If it's true for me, could it be true for you too?

IF I KEEP WAITING WELL IN THE MIDST OF PAIN, MY PERSEVERANCE PRODUCES CHARACTER, AND MY CHARACTER PRODUCES HOPE. AND THE WHOLE HORRIBLE, HOLY PROCESS PRODUCES CHANGE WORTH WANTING.

55

A LIFE WORTH LOVING

My fortieth birthday coincided with a family trip back to our old Los Angeles stomping grounds, so I seized the opportunity to plan a fabulous West Coast party. I enlisted several longtime LA friends to pitch in with food, flowers, and entertainment—delegation is my spiritual gift, after all!—and they did not disappoint. We gathered in a beautiful backyard on a clear, cool California night to celebrate forty years of good/hard living.

We wined and dined and laughed and cried. At my special request, my favorite vocalist (his name is Jay Wolf, ever heard of him?) even performed a short set list of songs. The night ended with a cupcake toast. In a rare display of extra-ness, I even got my hair and makeup done and hired a local photographer to capture the memories being made. The celebration was nothing short of perfect.

We returned home to Atlanta and quickly received the edited photos from the party. As I scrolled through the images, an unexpected wave of shock swept over me. It was quickly followed by an even more unexpected wave of grief. For myself, for my family, and for my dreams. Somehow, the objectivity of the photographs made the evidence of my suffering become so much more *real*.

To be clear, I had not spent a single moment of my youth dreaming of my fortieth birthday. To me, forty was a myth at best. I never could have imagined this was what forty would look like—or what *I* would look like. I stared at the final photo in the album, which pictured Jay and my two sons posing around me in my wheelchair. As viscerally wrong as the image seemed, I realized something: the woman in that photo wasn't perfect, but she sure was happy. Truly happy. She was surrounded by three people who loved her deeply, and every one of them was smiling. Even if my particular smile was a little bit crooked.

I could reject my reality, but what good would that do? *This is your life*, I told myself as I made one more pass through the photos, *so what if you decided to truly love it?*

I'll ask you the same question. What if you decided to truly love your life? To stare your reality in the face and accept that no one else is going to live it for you?

So I did. In a conscious move beyond mere acceptance, I am strategically narrating my life to myself with a generous emphasis on what is good. Just as I chose to see what was right in that birthday photograph, I am focusing on what's right in my life. Every day, I'm making an effort to name what's good about my work and my family and my home and my body, as if my life depends on it. Because in some ways it does. And whether you know it or not, yours does too.

Take a moment here. Pull up a photo or look around your home or just close your eyes and imagine your life. Where do you see goodness? What is deeply right, even in the midst of so much wrong? There is something there to truly love, and I want you to find it.

Now, we'd be foolish to allow this hopeful reframing to teeter into delusion or denial. I will never endorse ignoring what's deeply dysfunctional or downright wrong. But I am acknowledging that it's not a mistake that you and I are still here. It's not a mistake that our lives exist in the world. I am taking as much ownership as I can of living a life worth loving. Loving my life has helped me heal.

I think God intended me to be here. I also think He intends me to *enjoy* being here. When I finally began to believe that a good life doesn't have to be a pain-free life, I granted myself permission to truly, deeply, fully love the life right in front of me.

If it's true for me, could it be true for you too?

I CAN TAKE OWNERSHIP OF LIVING A LIFE WORTH LOVING.

56

RETURNING TO EL MATADOR

Dark storm clouds were gathering over the choppy gray ocean and moving with alarming speed toward the beach. I glanced up the zigzagging staircase, which linked El Matador Beach to a parking lot at the top of a steep cliff. About fifty friends of mine were hauling tents, tables, linens, food, and drinks—all the makings of my meticulously planned joint twenty-fourth birthday party with Jay on the most spectacular beach in Malibu. (Yes, my guests were doing all the manual labor. Follow me for more hosting hacks!) I simply couldn't believe that a rainstorm had the gall to ruin my perfectly planned party.

As our guests made their final trips down the cliff like so many pack mules, God bless them, it began to rain. More truthfully, it began to pour. I huddled with dozens of guests under our single (very small, very flimsy) tent and convinced myself the whole thing was a bust. Realizing the storm wasn't letting up anytime soon, the partygoers took off their shoes, shook out their wet hair, and danced in the rain to the tunes of Jay's carefully curated mix CD. (This was 2006, after all.) The night was incandescently dreamy.

Until my physical abilities were largely wiped out two years later, I had never once considered how physically demanding it was to take on the steep trail and hundred rickety steps to get down the cliff to El Matador. But later, as a disabled person, I was haunted by the thought of it. Would we ever be able to make the journey down to that special place again? Would our memories of those times on El Matador Beach remain only memories, fading like misty rain?

Six years, nearly to the day, after our birthday celebration at El Matador, we had another celebration on that very beach. And this one felt far more momentous than the first.

Jay's family was in town and, feeling particularly nostalgic, we all decided returning to El Matador should be on the itinerary. We stuffed ourselves into a couple of cars and made the hour-long drive to Malibu. When we arrived, my eyes widened and I choked down a cartoonishly loud *gulp* as I took in the path in front of me. Had the cliffside trail always been this steep and washed out? Or had I just had a stroke?

Jay referenced his rusty Spanish and reminded us that *el matador* technically translates to "the killer," which was exactly the heartening bit of trivia I needed to hear as we began our descent. I intertwined my arm with Jay's, and we slowly walked in tandem, receiving some much-needed backup from Jay's dad and sisters.

This time around, the journey from the parking lot to El Matador took me every bit of an hour, ten times as long as it ever had before my stroke. But the view from the bottom—craggy beach caves bordering foamy water that reflected the soft sunset and streaks of pink clouds—was as breathtaking as it had always been. Maybe even more, since I had assumed I'd never see it again.

As you and I have learned, God might not always bring you back to the places you've been (or, ahem, the volcanoes you once hiked). But sometimes He might beckon you back to the very place you never thought you'd see again. For me it was El Matador. But it was also motherhood and a career in public speaking. And once I got a second chance to make the hard journey back to these places, the views were more spectacular than ever.

Dreaming of returning to the places we love feels almost unbearably vulnerable. I bet you've been haunted by the experiences you once took for granted and tormented at the thought of never going back to them. But as scary as it might sound, I want you to keep your eyes and heart open for God's invitation to follow Him to the places you once loved. Maybe that means believing you can grow a healthy marriage after a divorce or take a tender step toward conception after infant loss. It might even be as simple as making it through the front door of a workplace or church or friend's home after suffering has made you into someone unrecognizable. Dear one, the journey back won't be easy, but you weren't made for the easy stuff. God might just hook His arm through yours and walk you back to the old places you've dreamed about. But this time He'll bring you back as someone new.

After conquering El Matador, and so many other "El Matadors" along the way, I'm convinced that sometimes the hardest, most perilous journeys end in the most spectacular moments. Sometimes the descents that should have killed us bring us to the deepest beauty and comfort we'll ever know. The path will likely be worn and steep, and you'll want to turn back to the way things were before you started. But that longed-for arrival at your landing place will be well worth every minute of the journey.

If it's true for me, could it be true for you too?

IF GOD BRINGS ME BACK TO THE OLD PLACES,
HE'LL BRING ME BACK AS SOMEONE NEW.

57

A BANQUET TABLE

T he long wooden banquet table was overflowing. Bright bowls of oranges, spilling clusters of plump grapes, piles of striped gourds, and silver goblets of wine were softly lit by glowing taper candles scattered throughout the spread. As I took in the feast before me, I was a little nervous to find out who would be sitting to my right and left. *I sure hope they like me! Hopefully the small talk won't be too awkward.*

I was not taking my assigned seat at a wedding reception or some fabulous fundraising gala. I was posing for a painted depiction of the Luke 14 parable, of all things. The ancient story follows a rich man who wanted to throw a party for all his fancy friends. He put in a ton of work to make the party unforgettable, but all his guests were too busy to come. Flaky folks are the worst. So instead of canceling the banquet, the rich man rounded up all the misfits who never got invited to parties and he hosted a gorgeous feast for them instead.

I was honored to be tapped as a subject of a modern-day rendering of the Luke 14 banquet, along with about twenty other people affected by disabilities. In no time at all, I learned that the woman seated to my right had survived an acid attack, which left her eyes and facial skin irreparably damaged. To my left, I met a woman who now lived with quadriplegia from a car accident that took the lives of her children.

Suddenly, my issues felt pretty insignificant. Heck, my situation seemed like a lifetime Caribbean cruise compared to the ones around me! I was almost embarrassed to be sitting at the same table as these people, to have my suffering considered on par with theirs. But as I continued chatting with my seatmates and with the other extraordinary subjects around the table, they each expressed sincere grief for my

TREASURES IN THE DARK / 122

circumstances that moved me to tears. Suffering hadn't shrunk their hearts, you see. It had expanded their capacity for compassion.

The more stories of suffering I hear, the more I understand that our humanity places each of us on a spectrum of suffering. The types of suffering may be different, but every point along the spectrum is still pain. None is more or less significant than the rest. Not yours. Not mine. While I'm all for gaining perspective on our suffering, ranking our pain against another's is a total waste of time. Instead, our experiences of suffering are best leveraged when they make us more aware of other people's pain. Suffering grants us the hard-won privilege of compassion.

I was so moved by my time at that table that I knew I had to throw a party of my own. A few years later, Jay and I would recreate a Luke 14 banquet as the finale to our very first week of Hope Heals Camp. Tables overflowing with good food and fresh flowers served as the meeting place for every kind of pain and the starting point for all kinds of compassion. This camp tradition—this high-resolution picture of heaven—continues to this day.

It's hard to believe, but your experience of suffering can actually get upgraded from a liability to an asset. It is more than possible. But to make that happen you've got to stop wishing for other people to care about your pain and start asking how your pain can help you care about other people. The shift is uncomfortable. But so is self-pity.

As I sat amid the bustle of that painting set, I relished my moment among the misfits. I paraphrased Eugene Peterson's opening to the Luke 14 parable in *The Message*: "How fortunate the one who gets to eat dinner in God's kingdom!" (v. 15). I am learning that God's kingdom, as it exists here and now, is not a place free of pain. It's a place where pain has given way to compassion. When my hurts can be a part of your healing, the pain can feel more like a privilege.

If it's true for me, could it be true for you too?

WHEN MY HURTS CAN BE A PART OF SOMEONE ELSE'S
HEALING, THE PAIN CAN FEEL MORE LIKE A PRIVILEGE.

58
WHO I'VE BECOME

I was sitting in the car's passenger seat with Jay at the wheel. He was driving me to my weekly counseling appointment and the car was quiet. Unusually so, in fact, since I'm the most talkative person Jay knows . . . and he's the most talkative person I know! However, my brain was too busy kneading out some tangled thoughts to offer any conversation out loud. I was preparing to sit down for an hour of talk therapy, and I wanted to make sense of my feelings about the upcoming anniversary of my stroke. Or, more accurately, I wanted to make sense of my *lack* of feelings.

I am not wired to hang out in the past, usually. But anniversaries force us to remember what has happened. And just as much, what will never happen again. When April 21 rolls around each year, I'm not exactly thrilled to recall the details of the day I almost died. I don't jump out of bed as if it's Christmas morning. The day is weird and somber, but even so, it has never fully devastated me.

I have friends who become nearly incapacitated on the anniversaries of the worst days of their lives. They might spend a week in bed or stop eating for a while or go silent for days. Honestly, those responses seem perfectly reasonable to me. Pain demands to be felt at some point, and we can't always choose how we will feel it. Which is why I couldn't help but wonder, en route to my counseling appointment, *Why am I okay today?*

I asked my counselor as much after Jay had walked me into her office and helped me get settled on the couch. From her armchair across the small room, she held my gaze for a long moment. After a big, deep breath, she responded.

"Our suffering can feel a little more bearable when we like who we've become because of it."

Are you as floored by this revelation as I was? As strange as it felt to acknowl-edge, I really do like who I have become since my stroke. And *because* of my stroke. God used the worst experience of my life to develop the best parts of who I am today. And that is as miraculous a phenomenon as my survival.

I think I feel sorry for the hypothetical version of Katherine who never had a stroke. In fact, I pity her far more than I pity the real version of myself, the Katherine who has significant disabilities and a grim neurovascular prognosis. If my life had been less challenging, I don't think my spirit would have had the opportunity to grow in resilience and trust and humility. If my life had been more charmed, I would probably have an outsize sense of entitlement and unhelpfully rigid expectations of what I deserve.

My friend, you have no idea how much I wish I could erase the worst day from your life and wipe that dreaded anniversary off your calendar. But that would mean undoing the person you've become because of that worst day. And what a loss that would be. If you're brave enough to do it, imagine the version of yourself who never got the chance to develop resilience or humility or openhandedness. And, if you dare, allow yourself to feel a little pity for all they're missing out on.

As I left that therapy appointment, the cloud of weird feelings surrounding the anniversary of my stroke didn't totally dissipate. But I finally had some words to put around it. I couldn't thank God for my stroke. But I sure could thank Him for what my stroke gave me. And I could thank Him for who my stroke made me. I could acknowledge both the gifts and the darkness, as well as the gifts *in* the darkness.

If it's true for me, could it be true for you too?

MY SUFFERING CAN FEEL A LITTLE MORE BEARABLE
WHEN I LIKE WHO I'VE BECOME BECAUSE OF IT.

PART THREE

FOR THE HOPING

Finding Our Lives in the Bigger Story

PRACTICE RESURRECTION

Jay's sister Sarah and her family live on a big green hill in the middle of a soybean field in rural Kentucky. The white walls of their farmhouse are filled with photographs and artwork and maps from their travels. There's one piece in particular I make a point to see whenever I visit their home—a framed letterpress print of a poem written by beloved Kentuckian Wendell Berry.

If a Venn diagram exists comparing that spicy octogenarian, agrarian activist and Katherine Wolf, the overlapping space at the center is pretty small. You might even need a microscope to see it. But the one thing Wendell and I do have in common is a dearly held belief in God's standing invitation to new life. The framed poem I always make sure to visit in Sarah's back hallway ends with a line so compelling it makes my heart flutter every time I read it: "Practice resurrection."[5]

For most of my life, these two words didn't go together as far as I could tell. I've been a heartfelt follower of Jesus ever since I can remember. Even as a little child, I could've told you the story of His life and death backward, forward, and upside down. Even so, I understood resurrection as a special, one-time-only event that validated the Christian faith and proved Jesus was God. It was an experience specific to the Savior, and I was supposed to marvel at it from afar.

But then I met death and was laid in my own tomb of sorts. Suddenly, I needed resurrection to be more than "something to believe in." Resurrection had to become a reality in my life, right then and there.

In a pale, slow-motion shadow of Jesus' resurrection, I eventually rose into a second-chance life of my own. My victory over death looked less like a rolled-away stone and more like being rolled away in a wheelchair. But I survived, and I am surviving, in the present tense. And now, on this side of near-death, I understand that's the most important part of resurrection: it's happening here and now. To you. To me. It's happening to all of us, if we choose to recognize it. To fight for it. To *practice* it.

Christ's redemptive work didn't begin and end the day He walked out of the tomb two thousand years ago. Jesus' second-chance life set into motion a staggered but certain rhythm of resurrection, echoing through reality: disappointment then delight, hard then good, wounding then healing, death then new life. That's the cycle we're all in.

In my life, practicing resurrection has been as grand a gesture as having another baby after my stroke. It's also been as mundane as choosing to get out of my bed—putting one foot down on the bedroom carpet, then the other—on days when hiding in the dark feels more appealing than showing up to my life, my work, my disabilities, and my family.

For you, the practice of resurrection might mean being brave enough to make the first move to reconcile a relationship you thought was long dead. It might mean hosting a fabulous birthday party for yourself smack in the middle of the worst year of your life. It might mean one more day of choosing sobriety and presence instead of numbing out. Or it might be as simple as allowing yourself to laugh, to smile, to feel even a fleeting moment of happiness when loss is weighing you down like lead shoes.

Resurrection is always available, but I don't think it's automatic. As we wade through the thickest parts of our suffering, new life beyond death feels as distant and abstract as that ancient, empty tomb Jesus busted open. In the months following my stroke—before I could walk, talk, eat, or care for my son—death actually seemed like a better option than whatever unknown life might lie ahead of me. Resurrection presents us with the risk of embarking on a new life we never expected to live, a life that will look altogether different from the one we had. Goodness, can I attest that the risk is worth it.

While my stroke didn't kill me, the losses it left me with seemed too heavy to bear—until I began reframing them as invitations to *practice resurrection*. To make space for surprising second chances and new life. To open up to the possibilities beyond my old life. When I began practicing resurrection in one area of my life, opportunities for second chances sprang up all around me—in my marriage, my friendships, my career, my health. Now, after a decade and a half of a present-tense practice of choosing new life, I understand that *persistent practicing of resurrection* is just different wording for *healing*.

If it's true for me, could it be true for you too?

I CAN REFRAME MY LOSSES AS OPPORTUNITIES TO JOIN IN JESUS' ONGOING PATTERN OF PRACTICING RESURRECTION.

The hydraulic platform groaned loudly as it cranked into upward motion, causing me to lurch off-balance. My head swam and I grasped for the arm of the man standing next to me. I felt like a passenger on an elevator without walls . . . which was precisely the situation I'd found myself in, I guess. A dizzy nausea washed over me, but I plastered on a big smile and prepared to deliver my lines.

It was my sophomore year of college, and I had been chosen as one of the two emcees for a beloved Samford University song and dance competition called Step Sing. That year, the production crew had gone all out and installed a mechanized lift that would raise my cohost and me from below the stage when the show began. Every miserable ride on that darn platform triggered bouts of vertigo like I'd never experienced before. *Am I pregnant?!* I wondered, despite knowing full well that I had done exactly zero things in all my life required to actually become pregnant.

The show went on because it had to. I managed the dizziness during every dress rehearsal and all three live performances—wearing a ball gown and heels, no less! When the show wrapped, I was eager to get a professional opinion on my symptoms, so I scheduled an appointment with a primary care physician. As I explained the dizziness, she scribbled on her clipboard and deftly managed to evade even a millisecond of eye contact with me. She interrupted me midsentence with a prescription for vertigo medication, then hustled me out of the clinic room.

Just a few years later, the dizziness—as well as a lifetime's worth of other mild neurological oddities—would all be explained when a malformation in my brain ruptured one April day. The arteriovenous malformation that almost killed me had been present since my birth, although I never knew about it. For years, it had been drop-ping clues of its existence that would only become apparent in retrospect.

What if I had seen a different doctor about the vertigo? What if an MRI had been ordered and the AVM identified while I was in college? What if I could have preempted the rupture with an elective surgery, rather than being blindsided by it? If I had known my brain was a ticking time bomb, would I have married Jay? Would I have gotten pregnant with James?

The multiverse of sliding-doors scenarios could drive me crazy if I let myself live there. The questions of what could have been and the anxieties of what could be are enough to incapacitate any of us. Taking up residence in the land of what if guaran-tees us either disappointment or spiraling. Or both . . . which is not great!

Hope is an escape hatch from the what-if loop because it gives you and me permission to live the lives we have. It narrows our vision to work with what's in front of us. Hope puts to rest all the lives we could have lived and gently reminds us, "This is the one you've got. Don't waste it." You could call it resignation, but I call it relief. Each day, you and I can decide to trade those anxious what-ifs for anticipatory what-ifs. Like, *What if none of this is an accident? What if God chose me for this? What if I start living like this is exactly the life I would have chosen?*

When spinning around the what-if loop makes me dizzier than any bout of ver-tigo, I make myself return to the life I actually have. I confront the reality of what has happened and choose to believe this reality was intended for me, whether I like it or not. I even dare to hope that this life and all its crazy-making specifics might just work together for some kind of good.

If it's true for me, could it be true for you too?

I CAN DECIDE TO TRADE ANXIOUS WHAT-IFS FOR HOPEFUL WHAT-IFS: *WHAT IF NONE OF THIS IS AN ACCIDENT? WHAT IF GOD CHOSE ME FOR THIS? WHAT IF I START LIVING LIKE THIS IS EXACTLY THE LIFE I WOULD HAVE CHOSEN?*

61

UNBURIED TREASURE

I'm almost always described as a "survivor" when introduced at speaking engagements or in interviews. For me, that word conjures up images of desert islands and death-defying feats of strength and hunting for food . . . Come to think of it, I'm just describing the TV show *Survivor*. But despite the fact that I'm often called a "survivor," I am actually not a very adventurous woman. Since life has required so much grit from me, risk for the sake of recreation could not seem less appealing to me. I've simply seen and survived too much.

My risk-loving, free-spirited naivete of youth got trampled under adulthood responsibilities and some hospital gurneys along the way. Not a day goes by that doesn't tempt me to protect and manage and fret over my life. Swaddling myself and my boys in Bubble Wrap seems more reasonable than risking life out there in an unsafe, unkind world.

Jesus once told a story of a rich man who, before leaving town, lent a bit of money to a few of his servants. A couple of the servants invested the money and ended up with more than what they'd originally been given. But one servant was so afraid of losing the money that he buried it in the ground for safekeeping (Matthew 25:14–30). Honestly, I get that.

Smarter people than I have interpreted that parable in many different ways. But to me, it sounds like a warning against holding your one precious life too tightly. Jesus was giving us permission to put all God has given us to good use. To invest it well. The world can feel too unsafe to risk the treasure of our lives. But what good is treasure if it's buried? Not much good at all.

Am I now inspired to skydive or take up motorcycle racing? Nope! But I have instated a life-affirming little ritual to remind myself I don't have to be afraid. Once a year at the beginning of summer, I find a waterslide wherever I may be and I slide down it. (A small set of pool stairs has even been known to work in a pinch!) It's not exactly death-defying, but Jay always films it in slow motion to make it feel a little more epic. For someone with a disabled body and a busted-up neurovascular system, it feels like a pretty grand declaration that I'm refusing to bury the treasure of my life. A reminder to invest the capital that's been given to me with some gumption. An affirmation of the truth that wisdom can mean taking a risk.

Do you ever get the sense you're burying your life under the pretense of wise stewardship or safekeeping? If so, let's imagine together what a good investment might look like for you. Maybe it's risking vulnerability in a friendship or pursuing that late-in-life career change. Maybe it's finally opening up to the possibility of love again.

Sadly, there will never be a shortage of things to fear as we move through this unsafe world. Fear often prevents us from getting out into the world at all, in fact. But at the very end, we may risk looking back on our too-safe lives to realize we didn't actually live them. And that would be something worth fearing!

The risk of loss is as inherent to a life well lived as it is to an investment wisely made. So, my friend, you and I have to get comfortable with the possibility of some disappointment and failure and grief along the way. That may just mean we're doing this whole thing right.

I don't want what has happened to me to prevent what could happen to me. I don't want to bury all this priceless treasure I've found just because that seems like the safest thing to do. I want to spend it well, with lavish joy and delight, on others and on myself, on people I love and people I hardly know. I want to slide feetfirst into the cool pool of new-to-me life, with loud whoops and hollers, leaving fear in my wake.

If it's true for me, could it be true for you too?

I CAN'T ALLOW FEAR OF LOSS TO PREVENT ME
FROM LIVING THE ONLY LIFE I HAVE.

WHAT THE LOCUSTS ATE

I spent my first Mother's Day totally unaware that it was Mother's Day. My stroke had occurred three weeks before, and I had become a mom just six months before that. My battered, foggy brain guaranteed I never would recover even a flicker of a memory from that day of my life, although a single photo was snapped. I'm pictured in the foreground—eyes closed, swollen head tilted back on my hospital pillow, and monitoring wires sprouting from my half-shaved scalp. At my bedside, Jay is holding a deliciously chunky baby James, who wears a onesie with the word *Mom* across the front. Even though I appear unconscious, my left hand is wrapped around James's little thigh.

Losing my ability and access to parent my infant son was, hands down, the most excruciating part of suffering a massive stroke. When I was still living in hospitals, family members would bring James to see me. But when nap time came or visiting hours ended, he would be taken away to a house that wasn't mine to be cared for by someone who wasn't me. When I was healthy enough to move into a house with Jay and James, my gait and coordination still lacked enough stability to allow me to safely care for James. I remember sobbing in my bed as I listened to James cry in his crib because I knew I could not walk into his room and hold him in my arms like most mothers could. The grief—and guilt—were unbearable. I had never known a spiritual famine as miserable as this one.

The first and second chapters of the book of Joel present a pretty grim—but scarily accurate—picture of what spiritual famine feels like in our lives. The prophet called those seasons "the years the locusts have eaten" (2:25). And old Joel didn't spare a colorful detail when it came to just how dry and dreadful those days of famine were for the Israelites. Food was scarce, the land was parched, and foreign armies threatened in every direction. Joel even said joy was "just a memory" (1:16 MSG). I mean, yikes. Does this sound kind of like the famine you've been through, or is it just me?

Then Joel told us the Israelites finally turned toward God in the midst of their suffering. They cried out to Him. They expressed their longing for restoration. And He delivered. He delivered so fully that no one could argue that God was anywhere but "in the thick of life with Israel" (2:27 MSG).

Dear one, I think what was true for the Israelites millennia ago is true for you and me too. God is waiting for us to turn toward Him, to trust Him with our dreams of healing and wholeness. He wants to show us that He's not just interested in survival; He's interested in life-to-the-thickest restoration.

We saved that *Mom* onesie from my first Mother's Day photo, even though the idea of having another child seemed impossible (even delusional) at the time. I couldn't care for the one I had, after all. But something compelled us to pack the little outfit away. Somewhere deep, deep, deep in my heart, I held on to the flicker of a dream and the whisper of a prayer that I might have another child. That the years the locusts ate might just be restored. That God might be good for His word. For a long time I didn't even dare put out-loud words around the particular hope of second-chance motherhood. But I nurtured a vision of what restoration might look like in my life. One day, I got the courage to share that vision with God.

Beloved, I know that the locusts have eaten away at the fullness of your life. You have starved. You know what famine feels like. But tell me this: What would restoration look like for you? Be specific. Offer God your detailed dreams of wholeness.

Of course, there's no magic in expressing these dreams to God. But there must be meaning in it, because He asks us to do it. In my life, restoration hasn't been granted like a wish. It's come in God's timing and in God's ways, not mine. If I'm being honest, it felt like He took His sweet time making it happen. But after eight long years, Jay would dig out that onesie and snap another Mother's Day photo, this time of my poststroke baby, John, wearing it on his first Mother's Day. In that moment the restoration was as thick as a baby's thighs. Take that, locusts.

For the record, my second-chance parenthood has been anything but simple or easy. The euphoric thrill of mothering my two boys was often brought back down to earth during a cross-country flight with an inconsolable toddler or some angst from our hormonal teen. I have yet to master any Zen-like tranquility or twinkle-in-my-eye gratitude as the family melts down every Thursday after school like clockwork. But, hey, nobody claimed restoration has to be perfect.

So much has been restored in my life, but truthfully I'm still waiting on some more. But this time I'm letting God in on the longing so that I'm not alone for the wait.

If it's true for me, could it be true for you too?

I CAN TRUST GOD WITH MY HOPES FOR RESTORATION.

FOR SUCH A TIME AS THIS

At a lanky six feet, six inches tall with clear blue eyes and a broad, good-humored smile, my father, Brooks, is an unmissable beacon of vitality and youthfulness. Even into his late sixties, he worked full-time (and full-force) in finance, maintained a lifelong running regimen, and tirelessly defended his title as the favorite goofball of his two grandsons.

After nearly fifteen years on the West Coast, Jay and I could no longer ignore the longing to return to the South to be closer to our families, my dad included. As we embarked on our final summer in Los Angeles—a summer full of packing boxes and saying goodbyes—my parents embarked on a much-anticipated European vacation. While abroad, my dad started experiencing an intense, widespread ache in his chest. My parents cut the trip short and returned home to Georgia with a calendar full of scans and consultations to determine the source of the pain.

In the midst of this slow-motion diagnostic process, Jay, the boys, and I drove across the country from California and began settling into our new chapter in Atlanta. No sooner had we unpacked the last moving box than my parents received a definitive diagnosis. My dad—my full-of-life dad—had multiple myeloma, a rare and aggressive form of cancer that affects the body's plasma cells. He was prescribed weekly infusion treatments in Atlanta, which meant our new guest bedroom was immediately put to its best and highest use as we began hosting him each Thursday night.

A few months later, on Christmas Day, my dad underwent a cutting-edge stem cell transplant that intentionally dragged him to the "basement" of health, where he got as close to death as possible before beginning a rebound. He also took a bad fall that same week, to add insult (and bruises) to injury. We spent our first Christmas in

Atlanta at his bedside in Emory University Hospital with a nearly unbearable front-row view to the pain and surrender demanded by his healing. This was not exactly the festive homecoming holiday I had imagined.

The timing felt so hurtful and deeply unfair. We'd moved back to the South to make new memories with our families, and—*bam!*—my dad gets diagnosed with cancer. *Come on! Can't we just catch a break?* we pleaded, maybe to God. Or maybe to the cancer.

If my own life has trained me to do anything, it's to find and to tell the truest story, the story of hope. I could have kept telling myself the story of my dad's diagnosis as if it were a disaster, but I wanted to tell it as if it were divine instead. We had moved back at just the right time to be with my parents when they needed us the very most. When I let hope determine my perspective, I realized my family had not spent such sweet moments of quality time together in recent memory. We had returned home for such a time as this, and I wasn't going to waste a minute of that time on self-pity.

You may have the choice between two versions of a narrative today. From experience, I can't recommend the hopeful version highly enough. Because when we tell the true versions of our stories, we can show up as the true versions of ourselves—as helpers instead of victims. If you can't quite find the thread of the divine story for yourself, ask God to take a highlighter to the truest parts of your life.

My dad's diagnosis had made us undeniably necessary to each other once again. In a full-circle cycle of redemption, I was able to show up for my dad at his hospital bedside, just as he had shown up so tirelessly at mine after my stroke. The true version of my story will never be the perfect version of my story, but it is the version that ends with redemption.

If it's true for me, could it be true for you too?

WHEN I TELL THE TRUE VERSION OF MY STORY, I CAN SHOW UP AS THE TRUE VERSION OF MYSELF—A HELPER, NOT A VICTIM.

THE NEXT BEST THING
TO TIME TRAVEL

What do you hope for the future?

That's probably a question you've been asked a time or two, perhaps during a job interview or on a first date. (Major green flag, by the way. Consider a second date for sure.) But have you ever been asked what you hope for the *past*?

Kind of a weird thought, huh? Because for most of us, hope is forward-facing and unidirectional. From *I hope this zit disappears before aforementioned second date* to *I hope the cancer treatment works*, we slap hope on anything and everything that's ahead of us and out of our control. We use it to soothe our present anxiety about an unknown future. But only recently did it occur to me to hope backward. To hope for the past.

We're stuck on a one-way road trip through time and space, so we can't help but approach the past as something fixed and decided. Our only real loophole is remembrance. While it doesn't allow us to materially change any of our choices or their outcomes, remembrance can help us change the way we *think* about our past, even if all the specifics remain the same. Doesn't that take the pressure off? A moment doesn't have to be perfect or to-plan to eventually be remembered as important, useful, or good. I'm no quantum physicist, but I think hopeful remembrance might just be the next best thing to time travel!

The longer I live inside my good/hard story, the more I see the past as malleable and layered. If the past is set in stone, it's less like a slab of hard slate and more like an opal: iridescent with streaks of color and light—previously hidden—flashing into sight as I view it from new angles.

For me, the spiritual practice of hope looks like recognizing all the glints of undeserved provision, opportunities for redemption, and unexpected beauty threaded through my life. Practically speaking, these reflections usually take the form of using a few moments each week to write some stream-of-consciousness thoughts about an old experience. Before I start, I ask God to open my mind and heart to new possibilities for the past. Nine times out of ten, a beautiful new truth or encouraging insight rises from a dusty old story. Miraculously, my past produces something new. This little ritual may give you the impression that I have my life together, but don't be fooled. "Writing" for me means dictating a typo-riddled run-on sentence into my phone, then immediately losing all those revelations in the wasteland of my Notes app. So take heart; you can do this too.

Viewing the past with hope should never obscure the pain or bypass the hurt we've experienced. Authentic hope fully embraces the broken stuff. Then it helps us mend those fractured pieces into something greater than the sum of their parts. Hope links the past to the present and the present to the future. We recognize the redemption of the past, so we accept the complexities of the present and look forward to the goodness of the future.

I'm revisiting my past like a time traveler bent on hope. Sometimes that means reexamining childhood wounds and wonders. Other times it means choosing to immediately reframe the very day I've just lived. Hopeful remembrance allows us endless new versions and fresh views of our lives, with no expiration date. I find that hope points to a future promise, lived out in the present, that gives purpose to my past.

If it's true for me, could it be true for you too?

HOPE IS A FUTURE PROMISE, LIVED OUT IN THE PRESENT, THAT GIVES PURPOSE TO MY PAST.

A LIBRARY OF LIVING SURVIVAL GUIDES

Side-by-side rocking chairs sway back and forth on a cabin porch as two new camp friends talk and laugh together. This idyllic little scene, captured in one of my all-time favorite photographs, is about as quintessential "summer camp" as it gets. That is, until you notice each of the subjects is missing his legs from the knees down.

Jude, who is about seven years old in the photo, lost significant parts of both his legs in a lawn mower accident when he was a toddler. Before his first summer at Hope Heals Camp, Jude hadn't met many people without their legs and was shyly ecstatic to meet his fellow camper Doug, who had become an amputee in his thirties after surviving a fluke forklift accident on a job site.

This moment summed up exactly why I'd been so determined to create a space where people could find flesh-and-bones proof that suffering wasn't the end of their story. I wanted to compile a library of survival guides where every Jude could find a Doug. And where every Doug could find a Jude! Gathering hundreds of people with disabilities in rural Alabama isn't the most logical operation (let's be real, it's a total logistical nightmare), but efficiency pales in comparison with the opportunity to foster a compassionate, inter-ability community.

Summer after summer, Jude and his family joined us as campers until the year they decided to attend as volunteers. This dear family took their roles as survival guides seriously and felt compelled to pass on the healing they had received to campers who were walking through the thick of hurting.

A few summers ago at the annual camp talent show, to a crowd of hundreds of misty-eyed listeners, Jude recited a poem he had written. In a quiet voice, he read:

> We shouldn't be ashamed of our bodies, like if we are black or
> white. We are all made in the image of God, like in Genesis
> chapter two, verse twenty-five. "And the man and his wife
> were both naked and were not ashamed [ESV]." But when Adam
> ate the fruit, then they saw they were naked. And they were
> ashamed. Let's put it this way: even if you have no feet, don't be
> ashamed if someone says something. Like, "Gross, put your feet
> back on." Maybe they haven't seen someone without feet.

Those are the words of someone who knows there is wholeness beyond the hurting. Someone who has seen purpose in their pain. Jude found a survival guide in Doug. And now he is becoming a survival guide in his own right.

Sure, we've all gotta survive for ourselves. But, to me, surviving for the sake of other people is a lot more motivating. Dear one, it's possible for your journey into the darkness to blaze a trail for someone else in their own wilderness. Could you believe me when I say your pain doesn't have to be wasted? Your pain can serve a lifesaving, heart-changing, soul-healing purpose. And doesn't that make you think about your suffering in a whole new way?

The pain of my suffering has touched so many people beyond myself, but my healing has too. When I freely share my story, I can be a part of seeing a generation of hurt give way to a generation of hope. Suffering is not the end of my story; rather, it's the beginning of a survival guide that I want to share with anyone who needs it.

If it's true for me, could it be true for you too?

MY JOURNEY IN THE DARKNESS CAN BLAZE A TRAIL
FOR SOMEONE ELSE IN THEIR OWN WILDERNESS.

66

CARPE DIEM

W hat's the worst that could happen?"

Jay and I asked ourselves that question a lot in the year 2014. I had recently undergone a pretty intense brain surgery to remove an aneurysm, totally unrelated to my stroke in 2008, that was located on the "good" side of my brain. While the success of the operation made it possible for us to consider having another baby, the logistics of pregnancy, delivery, and new motherhood in a disabled body seemed daunting and risky, to put it mildly.

Suffering, I've noticed, is capable of causing two dramatically different reactions. It can tempt us to hide within the safe walls of our homes and cower behind the status quo. Or it can push us out into a bold *carpe diem* confrontation of the world. (If you just heard Robin Williams's voice in your head, let's be friends.)

In months of circular conversations about growing our family, Jay and I always landed in the same place. God had given us this second chance, so we'd be foolish not to live it. And live it with some *umph*! We'd survived the worst day of our lives and then made it far enough to see a whole lot of good days. Constantly mitigating risks wouldn't prevent pain. I was making a lasagna when I had my stroke, for goodness' sake! That's not exactly daredevil behavior.

One afternoon in 2014, Jay and I visited our friends Lisa and Eric. Years earlier, before we knew her, Lisa had lost nearly all use of her limbs with the sudden onset of a rare neurological disorder called transverse myelitis. Literally overnight, she had become a quadriplegic. With signature New Yorker grit, Lisa relearned to drive in an adapted car, completed her master's degree, and founded a nonprofit organization for under-resourced youth in her neighborhood. To top it all off, she'd recently given birth to a baby girl, who bounced on Eric's lap as we hung out on their front porch.

"Katherine, if I can do this, so can you," Lisa encouraged me. "We can handle hard things. We've already proved it!"

Lisa was right. We could handle hard things, and boy, did God deliver. In the summer of 2015, I gave birth to John Nestor Wolf. We've known few joys deeper than being John's parents . . . and we've known few challenges more humbling than being John's parents. Now eight years old, our explosive "John Bomb" has mellowed into more of a festive confetti cannon. But the teenage years are still ahead. Pray for us.

My near-death experience took me by my shoulders and shook me out of the daze of ordinary life. It shouted, "This is all you get, so why aren't you living like it?" If you've bumped into death, I bet it asked you the same question. What's waiting to be seized on this very day of your second-chance life? Just as I asked myself so many years ago, I want you to tell me: What's the worst that could happen? I bet the worst thing isn't worth hiding out forever to avoid.

Don't misunderstand me. I did not jet out of the intensive care unit on a motorized wheelchair, ready to become the world's first half-paralyzed stuntwoman. It was years before Jay, James, and I dared to venture out into a world that felt unknown, unsafe, and unwelcoming to us. But after a season of cocooned healing, we slowly waded into a new normal and a new-to-us world. I'd lost the innocent illusion that bad things would never happen to me. But in return I'd gained enough clarity and confidence to seize my life like someone who could handle anything that came her way.

If it's true for me, could it be true for you too?

SUFFERING CAN INVITE ME INTO A BOLD *CARPE DIEM* EXPERIENCE OF THE WORLD.

67

REBELLION

We bought our first home in early 2010, over five years after we were married and just shy of two years after my stroke. From our first subleased furnished apartment in Hollywood (which made me cry, in a bad way, the first time I saw it) to our law school dorm to temporary hospital-adjacent housing, each of our previous living situations had been more utilitarian than hospitable. We'd made do with hand-me-down furniture that would make any DIYer beam with pride. Now we were eager to create a space of our own. Knowing my time in the residential neuro rehab facility would soon come to an end, we began the search for a home in the ridiculously quaint Los Angeles neighborhood of Culver City.

We still had no idea what life was going to look like. At that point, I wasn't even able to swallow food or liquids. Nonetheless, we zeroed in on a little yellow bungalow with high hopes of living a normal life again soon. Only after the purchasing process had begun did we realize we did not own a single piece of furniture. Granted, the house wouldn't hold much more than a single piece of furniture. Even so, Jay began his search for a few necessities. He popped into a furniture store that he'd browsed whenever we visited Culver City and came upon the gorgeous round oak dining table we'd been eyeing even before my stroke.

Would I ever be able to enjoy a meal at this table? He didn't know. But was the table on sale? *Yes, yes it was.* That seemed like a good enough reason to buy it on the spot.

Jay doesn't recall spiritualizing the decision much. He didn't clock the moment as a significant gesture of faith. But in hindsight, we both see the purchase was an act of rebellion against fear. With enormous vulnerability, Jay risked gut-wrenching disappointment by believing that good days and good meals were ahead for me. Personally, I wouldn't have paid quite so much for the sake of symbolism. But I'm sure glad Jay did.

The table sat in a storage unit for several months as I continued daily swallowing therapy in residential rehab. Eventually, I passed my swallowing test and was given the green light to eat again. While so many physical deficits still lingered, I felt altogether healed after sitting down to our first family meal around that beautiful oak table the night we moved into our little yellow cottage.

Years later, the table moved with us to Atlanta. A little worse for wear (and covered in Sharpie scribble-scrabble from an up-and-coming artist named John Wolf), that table still serves as the central gathering spot of our home. Well over a decade later, I cannot look at it without remembering the power and importance of joyfully defying fear however I can, whenever I can.

Friend, no matter how tight a grip fear may have on you today, I know you are capable of rising up against it. Buy that bouquet of grocery store flowers for yourself instead of waiting for someone else to do it. Register for that race you can't imagine completing. Plan that trip in faith that your heart may soon be healed enough to enjoy the big wide world again. Find some way to rebel.

Do all my displays of rebellious faith end with a tidy, happy resolution? Of course not! And neither will yours. But I have developed so much courage in continuing to joyfully rebel against the outcomes that scare me most. These rebellions of the soul, whether big or small, remind me that goodness is ahead and that God is not confined to the constraints of reason. I'll reap the rewards when I'm brave enough to risk the vulnerability of rebelling against fear.

If it's true for me, could it be true for you too?

I REBEL AGAINST FEAR WHEN I TAKE ON THE RISK OF LIVING LIKE THERE ARE GOOD DAYS AHEAD OF ME.

68

SAVING THE
GOOD STUFF

Weddings in the South are serious business. Not one person down here has ever used the words *small* or *intimate* in the same sentence as *wedding*. Every sorority sister, neighbor, church member, elementary school teacher, fifth cousin, and grocery store cashier you've ever had will be invited to your wedding, should you have one in the South.

As I learned from my season of engagement in 2004, for every wedding guest there is a wedding gift. This equation produces what can only be described as a sinful abundance of loot. I participated in a very real and very long-standing tradition of displaying my gifts in my parents' home for months so that the ladies of Athens, Georgia, could come by and look at them like a particularly boring museum exhibit. Even though I'd do things pretty differently now, I'm still deeply moved by the culture of communal celebration and generosity.

Our wedding gifts ranged from the practical to the extravagant. And when you're twenty-two, just about any household gadget or set of linen napkins seems extravagant. I'd just vacated a twelve-by-twelve college dorm room made of cement blocks, for goodness' sake. The leap from those T-shirt sheets to embroidered Egyptian cotton seemed a bit daunting!

A couple of months after we married, Jay and I followed our dreams westward to California. Even though we didn't have a single piece of furniture to our names, we had to rent a full-size box truck just to schlep all our wedding gifts with us across the country. As we settled into our first little apartment, I found myself storing so many of our beautiful presents in the out-of-reach cabinets or in boxes under our bed.

Those crisp monogrammed sheets will be perfect when we have a real house, I thought. *Our usual home-cooked meals don't seem fancy enough for that silver platter, so we'll save it for a nice dinner. I'll burn that candle when we have guests over sometime soon.* All those special gifts would gather dust for the next two years, and then I would nearly die and lay unconscious in an intensive care unit while Jay and his mom packed them all into cardboard boxes the day after his law school graduation.

I eventually transitioned from the ICU to a series of rehab facilities. After a few months in my final residential rehab, I was permitted to start sleeping at the little house Jay was renting nearby. My first night at the house—which was the first night in months I would be sleeping in something other than a hospital bed—Jay had the inspired idea to dig out those monogrammed sheets from our hastily packed moving boxes and put them on the bed. Turns out, Egyptian cotton is way better than those T-shirt sheets.

Are you saving any good stuff in your life for later? When do you think "later" will finally arrive? I often catch myself with the stingy impulse to save the good stuff for when "real life" begins. I think that habit is less about frugality and more about ingratitude. Withholding the good stuff means, for some reason, I don't believe my life here and now is worthy of beauty, care, and delight. And what an insult that must be to the God who gave it to me. But the truth is my life is worth the good stuff! Even more so than any "later" that may be ahead for me.

Jay and I have found a surprising element of healing by choosing to really live, even in the midst of what feels like dying. The living usually looks small and a little ordinary but, goodness, does it work wonders. To this day, and even on our worst days, we usually eat dinner off our wedding china. We keep scented candles burning around the house, even if no one is visiting. And we always—*always*—sleep on the good sheets. And so should you.

I'm not guaranteed tomorrow, much less some nebulous point in the future when suffering might end so "real life" can begin. I want to live each day like the gift that it is by taking full advantage of the gifts I've been given.

If it's true for me, could it be true for you too?

I CAN CHOOSE TO *REALLY LIVE* IN THE MIDST
OF WHAT FEELS LIKE DYING.

69

NEW YORK, NEW ME

The last time I visited New York, I was a freshly engaged twenty-two-year-old. I'd traipsed through Central Park, navigated the subway with confidence, and sobbed my way through back-to-back musicals. I could do anything I wanted to do with total ease. Yet I hadn't even realized it.

Fifteen years later, Jay and I wanted to return to New York to celebrate our son James's twelfth birthday. For months before the trip, we planned all the details carefully. These credit card points would pay for that hotel room. Tickets to these strategically chosen shows would allow us to hit a matinee and an evening showing, all in one day! If we woke up early enough, we could eat five fabulous meals instead of just three. (Don't judge.) In true Wolf fashion, we were going to max this thing out, even if it killed us.

It took about five minutes of being back in the city to realize I was not the person I'd been during my last trip to New York. First of all, I was old now. (Why does everything have to be so loud there? Is it just me?!) Second, and most strikingly, my body simply wasn't capable of doing many of the things I wanted to do.

Navigating the crowded, uneven sidewalks in my wheelchair felt perilous, both for me and for innocent pedestrians. Finding a subway stop with an elevator proved even more difficult than flagging down an accessible taxi. And sitting through three hours of a musical with double vision and a deaf ear was almost nauseating. New York was beginning to feel less like a city of dreams and more like the place of my nightmares!

My pity party was in full tilt as I enumerated the experiences I'd never have again. Even more intensely, I worried I was holding back James and Jay from having the trip they deserved. But as I watched my wide-eyed boy take in the magic and madness of this new-to-him place, I realized I could give him something so much richer than a birthday trip. I could give him the example of someone who leaned wholeheartedly into all that she *could* do, rather than lamenting what she couldn't do.

When you look at your life today, what do you see first: All the things you can't do or all that you can do? And can be? And can enjoy and conquer and sink into? Friend, you can mourn all you've lost. But in the mourning, don't lose all that you still have.

I tackled the remainder of our New York trip with renewed vigor. We stuffed our faces with schmeared bagels and greasy pizza and world-famous cupcakes. We teared up in front of a few artistic masterpieces and pretended to be smart enough to understand the others. We strolled (and rolled) through Central Park and relished every one of the billion red-orange leaves.

It turns out, remembering what we don't have can also remind us of what we do have. Experiencing what we can't do can also remind us of what we can do. I may not be able to do it all, but goodness, I can do an awful lot. Even in the midst of near-constant loss, I never want to forget that my second-chance life is the one right in front of me. It's happening here and now. And I don't want to miss it.

The question becomes, "Here is my real life. It's not the one I used to have or the one I wished for, but it is the one that's mine. So what will I do with it?" The answer? Everything I possibly can, with my whole heart, until the very end.

If it's true for me, could it be true for you too?

I WON'T ALLOW REMEMBERING WHAT I'VE LOST
TO MAKE ME FORGET WHAT I STILL HAVE.

HANDWRITTEN HOPE

I have a dark secret I need to get off my chest. For as long as I can remember, I've had a terrible habit that I just can't seem to shake. I am addicted to stationery.

I've never met a method of communication I didn't like. Phone calls, coffee dates, passed notes, messages left on Facebook walls (remember those?!)—I'll take it all. But the supreme form of correspondence, without contest, is the handwritten note. Whether a birthday card scrounged from the Target sale rack or the finest personalized note card from a world-renowned *paperie*, I am obsessed with stationery.

You can find it in my purse, stuffed into my office cabinets, and tucked into my nightstand drawers. At this point, roughly 80 percent of our marital conflict can be traced back to Jay suggesting I do a little purge of my hoard. But that'll never happen! I'll continue to hang on to each absurdly niche piece until the perfect occasion aligns with the perfect recipient. I might even be buried with some of it.

There was a time when this lifelong affinity became a near impossibility. After my stroke, I lost fine motor control of my right hand, which was slightly inconvenient since I am, in fact, right-handed. Losing the ability to jot a quick handwritten note nearly devastated me. That specific loss felt cruelly symbolic of all the other ways my communication with the world had been cut off.

Over the past decade and a half, I've worked relentlessly to rewire my brain so I can learn to do old tasks in a new way, including writing with my left hand. The process has been incredibly frustrating and even a bit embarrassing. In the early days of my recovery, people often mistook my handwriting for my son's. And his handwriting was, ahem, not great.

Today, my writing still looks a bit like it was scratched out by a chicken. But at least I get to be the chicken in this scenario, and I'm pretty proud of that! My wobbly lines of letters tell the story of someone who shouldn't be alive to tell (or write) her tale, but she is. Because I have to concentrate on forming literally each and every shape, a handwritten note from me has a lot more than ink in it. It is filled with love and grit and proof that the recipient is worth every drop of the effort.

This pattern spins out into every other part of life. From unsteadily baking muffins for my boys to navigating airports in a wheelchair to slowly reading emails with my severe double vision, everything about my life is harder than it used to be. But it turns out, all the good stuff is still worth doing. And that means my stationery habit will continue to go unchecked. And Jay will simply have to be okay with that. We can have an organized home office when we're dead!

In this life after suffering, you have to try so much harder to show up. But, beloved, your showing up is sacramental. Your efforts are a prayer. Because when you keep putting in the effort to engage the goodness of life, you're writing God a thank-you note for what remains. And He knows it isn't easy to write.

Limitations can either stop us from doing the things we love or make us love those things even more. On the other side of loss, frustration, and embarrassment waits a deeper experience of worth and gratitude. It's from that place that I get to overflow with hope into a world that needs my message so desperately.

If it's true for me, could it be true for you too?

WHEN EVERYTHING ABOUT MY LIFE BECOMES HARDER
TO DO, I'LL LEARN WHAT'S TRULY WORTH DOING.

A NEW KIND OF CALLING

D id anyone else spend their early years all but agonizing over discovering God's "personal plan" for their life? In my memory, discovering our callings was a semi-obsessive focus of youth group sermons and Sunday school lessons for most of the nineties. I kept hearing that God had a plan for me, but no one told me exactly where I'd find it. Surely, I had missed a memo or something.

While the specifics were pretty fuzzy, I was certain I wanted to tell God's story in a public way. Remember, I spent many afternoons of my childhood pacing in front of a captive audience of baby dolls and unloading impassioned sermons. I knew this was my purpose, but I never imagined I'd do it from a wheelchair.

To our credit, most of us earnestly hope to use our lives in a way that honors God. But in our well-intentioned pursuits of His purpose for us, we may start to believe that an obstacle course lies between us and some mysterious, specialized calling from on high. Realizing your life's purpose can quickly become about proving just how clever, capable, and talented you can be. Which is kind of missing the point.

We tend to determine our capital-P Purpose by our strengths and abilities, rather than our weaknesses and constraints. While this line of reasoning is understandable, it could trick us into seeing only liabilities in our limitations, rather than opportunities for God's creativity. We fail to ask ourselves if God would even need to be all that powerful or creative to use capable people to accomplish His purposes.

As I walk further into the upside-down kingdom of God, I'm noticing a pattern: those for whom God writes the most amazing stories are often the least impressive characters. Some examples I especially love include:

Rather than choosing any one of the strong, experienced men in the land, God handpicked a teenage shepherd named David to lead His chosen people. (No offense to teenage boys—I have one!—but this was a weird choice.)

After Joseph was abandoned by his family and enslaved in a foreign country, God allowed him to become one of the most influential leaders in all of Egypt.

God chose an unwed teenage girl to deliver Jesus into the world. God trusted the Messiah, history's greatest treasure, into the care of someone without many obvious credentials.

And speaking of Jesus, He didn't visit earth as some divine tourist. He embraced every limitation and weakness of being human. In fact, He was called to be constrained so He could show us how to live.

God prefers to work within limitations, it seems, because those limitations prove just how unstoppable His power is. Limitations and calling are not opposing forces at war with one another. Rather, they are positive and negative spaces, dancing together to form a complete design. Maybe our limited energy should be invested into doing our "creative best" within our limitations (Galatians 6:5 MSG), rather than overcoming them.

Perhaps God will appoint me to a position of immense influence, or maybe He'll ask me to live a common life filled with uncommon grace. I'm starting to see that both are a calling. The more I know of God, the more my physical limitations invite me to release my mental limitations of what (and who) God will use to heal the world. I'm expanding my concept of calling to include my constraints as necessary parts of God's plan, rather than obstacles to be overcome.

If it's true for me, could it be true for you too?

I CAN FOCUS ON DOING MY "CREATIVE BEST" WITHIN MY LIMITATIONS RATHER THAN OVERCOMING THEM.

72
THE MIRACLES WE MISS

As I've mentioned before, our second son, John, was born a little over seven years after my stroke. In so many ways, his birth was as unlikely as my survival. Since the moment I found out I was pregnant, we've called John our miracle baby. I firmly believe that every new life—and old life and middle-aged life!—is a miracle. But a life sparked from the ashes of a near-death experience feels particularly special.

It took years of second-chance motherhood to realize that while John was a bona fide miracle child, he wasn't my first miracle child. Our oldest son, James, was born just six months and five days before my stroke. We would later find out that the congenital brain malformation that ruptured in April 2008 was present and had already begun slowly rupturing on the day James was born in 2007.

There's no discernible reason why my stroke didn't happen during the strain of my unmedicated delivery of James. Which makes James our first miracle baby. A miracle baby who now towers at a gangly six feet tall and shaves (shaves, people!) before catching the bus to high school.

How many other miracles have you and I missed? Which moments—and people—become miracles only with the clarity and context offered by time? When else have we confused the miraculous with the commonplace?

A million quiet miracles preceded my "big" miracles. The practice of searching my memory for those miracles-before-the-miracle feels like a treasure hunt. Once I shine the light of hope on the rubble—or even the simple ordinariness—of my life, God's provision and presence shine like a cavern of diamonds being hit with lantern light. When I look long enough, the miracles of Divine Love glitter everywhere. I am rich with them. I bet you are too.

Searching for miracles hidden in the past sets us up to recognize the miracles happening today, however softly or slowly. What feels normal now may prove to be supernatural with enough time. And what feels painful today might someday feel more like a privilege.

Friend, let's go on a little treasure hunt. Grab your lantern lit with the light of hope and take just a moment to trek back into your personal history. Think about the big, obvious miracles first. Now move that lantern closer to the stuff that looks ordinary. Can you see any little miracles hidden there that you've never noticed before? Once you start seeing them in the past, I can all but guarantee you'll see them all around you in the present. It won't be hard to live with a little more wonder and a lot more gratitude when miracles surround you wherever you go.

With each new day, I can continue the treasure hunt for evidence of God's love—however hidden—in the past and right here in the present.

If it's true for me, could it be true for you too?

WHEN I FIND MIRACLES IN THE ORDINARY PARTS OF MY PAST,
I START SEEING MIRACLES ALL AROUND ME IN THE PRESENT.

73

MORE WHOLE

My friend Penny, who has Down syndrome, recently taught me something deeply refreshing about how to see suffering. It was tucked into her response to a question.

Her mom asked her, "Penny, do you think you'll have Down syndrome in heaven?"

Penny looked at her mom for a moment with a furrowed brow. Then her face broke into a smile. She laughed. "I don't know! But that's a funny question."

This sincere and unpretentious response to a version of the age-old question of suffering disrupted so many of my long-held beliefs and assumptions about God, pain, and goodness. If that question had been directed at me—"Katherine, will you still wear the evidence of your stroke in heaven?"—I probably wouldn't have even paused to think before blurting out, "Are you crazy? Of course not!"

There are as many theories about heaven as there are people who believe in heaven, so I'm not in the business of speculating on specifics here. But I think we all can agree that heaven will be a place of wholeness. When I take some time to really imagine my eternal soul existing without evidence of my stroke, I don't really feel more whole. I actually feel a lot less whole.

What do I do with that?

Sitting around making bets on heaven doesn't feel like a great use of time. (Although, for the record, I do think we'll have cake for breakfast every day. Pretty sure that's in the book of Titus or something.) But I do think asking certain questions about heaven—and, really, about wholeness—can invite us into a new way of seeing our here-and-now hurt.

Penny's simple response to a philosophically dense question invited me to con-tinue exploring the darkness with curiosity and openhandedness. She offered me a generous new way of envisioning wholeness. I think suffering itself is the product of a not-right world. It's not from God, but He does intervene in it because He loves us and doesn't want us to be alone in the dark. Somehow, He keeps reaching into our not-right world to pull out something deeply right, which makes me wonder if all this suffering might just be a step toward the deepest kind of wholeness.

Dear one, your experience of suffering is singular and so complex. I would never dare to prescribe some simplistic theological answer here. But I will ask some ques-tions. What wholeness would you lose if the worst thing hadn't happened? What would your soul look like without the evidence of your suffering?

I'd like to think heaven does more than return us to the factory settings. If that were the case, we should have just stayed in the factory, am I right?! Instead, I think heaven is where our patinas of good/hard living will look their best. Where every layer of growth and grit and grace will be called *beautiful. Perfect. Whole.*

Would I reroute my own story of suffering and skip the stroke so I could regain my physical independence? To borrow Penny's words: "I don't know!" But I do know that any "regaining" would come with some undeniable loss. The best parts of me were born from the worst thing that ever happened to me. A lot of my "rightness" came out of what was not right.

If it's true for me (and Penny), could it be true for you too?

THE BEST PARTS OF ME CAN COME FROM THE
WORST THING THAT EVER HAPPENED TO ME.

74

THE BIRTHDAY FEAST

I share a birthday week with three phenomenal women who have faced equally phenomenal hardships. In recent years, we've established a tradition of commemorating another year of our lives—lives that none of us would have chosen—with a fabulous birthday lunch.

Ann, who sat to my left at this year's birthday feast, is a few years older than I am, to the day. Ann has two children with cystic fibrosis and wholeheartedly gives herself to advocating for her kids every single day. Shortly after meeting her, I remember feeling certain we had known each other since childhood, that she must have walked my pre- and poststroke journey with me. It turns out she's just a kindred spirit who knows as well as I do that deep pain and joy can coexist.

To my right sat Louisa and Harriet, beautiful sisters who both live with an ultra-rare degenerative neurological disease. Growing up, these young women were typical by all the accepted metrics. In their early adulthoods, when most young people are launching into the world independently, Harriet and Louisa received their diagnoses and began the slow process of grieving the independence they would never have. At this year's birthday lunch, their wonderful mother joined us.

Truthfully, we stuck out a bit. Two walkers and a wheelchair were parked next to our booth, and a few of us at the table needed some help cutting our food. Our conversation bounced from therapy appointments to wheelchair recommendations to insurance woes. Typical "ladies who lunch" stuff, you know?

I imagine our table was a curious and sobering sight for the diners and staff. By the looks of it, most of those people could have driven themselves there. They were able to swallow their food smoothly and the waitstaff walked independently from table to table to take lunch orders. Significant suffering undeniably distinguished our table from the rest of the crowd. As I looked around at the fancy people in this fancy restaurant, I began to feel some shame about our differences. I was tempted to try to hide our pain. *Maybe we should have just had lunch in the privacy of my kitchen where no one could stare*, I found myself thinking.

But before I got very far down that path of reasoning, our server delivered the delightful news that the bill had been covered anonymously. Where I saw a group of sufferers who stood out, a kind stranger saw a group of survivors who deserved celebrating.

Beloved, if your suffering has separated you from the crowd, shame off you. Yes, God has set you apart, but He doesn't want to humiliate you. He wants to honor you, and I pray He makes that clear to you every single day. Will you join me in stewarding our set-apart-ness well in refusing to hide the hurt from people who don't yet understand? Will you join me in proudly celebrating the lives we have, not the ones we thought would be? Because that's exactly what the world could use most.

Every last one of us will suffer someday—even all those fancy people in that fancy restaurant—so nothing could be more useful than seeing it done well. So let's show off some fabulous celebration in the midst of deep pain. Gratitude for the process, not the outcome. Radical ownership of the stories we've been given.

As I blew out the single candle atop my cupcake, I didn't wish for a normal life that blended into the crowd. I simply gave thanks for the sacred, set-apart life I have the honor of celebrating each and every day.

If it's true for me, could it be true for you too?

GOD IS SETTING ME APART—NOT TO
HUMILIATE ME BUT TO HONOR ME.

75

REVERSE CHAPLAINS

Few experiences in my life have proven more humbling than a regression to near-total physical dependence on other people at age twenty-six. After my stroke I trudged through years as a care-receiver, leaning on friends and family to drive me places, do many of the household chores, travel with me to speaking engagements, take care of my kids, and push my wheelchair. Jay Wolf still shaves my armpits, for goodness' sake! You have not experienced true humility until your groom takes on your underarm grooming.

It took me years to see myself as anything but a burden to my husband and the many other caregivers in my life. My relationships felt off-balance as I lived with the shame of needing near-constant assistance. Even worse, I assumed I could offer nothing of value in return.

As I sank more deeply and wholeheartedly into communities of suffering people, I got a heaping dose of secondhand hope and hard-won wisdom from my new peers. I spent time in the company of entire families living with the daily realities of disabilities, with parents who had buried children, with young adults clawing their way back to life after a world-shattering injury. If I listened closely enough, I realized these people were speaking a distinct language in which *hard* wasn't necessarily bad and *dependence* wasn't something to be pitied.

In fact, in this wonderfully upside-down place, physical dependence reflects our most real dependence, a deep need for God and each other. In the ecosystem of Divine Love, caregivers and care-receivers are not mutually exclusive categories. Those labeled "wounded" and "unwell" offer a kind of reverse ministry to the able-bodied and "unbroken."

Imagine seeking out a hospital bedside when you're hungry for hope or looking for true wholeness in a bereaved heart. Imagine seeing scars as glorious reminders of resilience, rather than covering them in shame. According to Jesus, this is exactly what we should be doing. "Blessed are those who mourn," He said (Matthew 5:4). The last will be made first (Matthew 20:16). Divine Love hovers near to the broken-hearted (Psalm 34:18).

From where I sit, the kingdom of God seems to belong to the reverse chaplains. Dear one, I've resented my role as a care-receiver for longer than I'd like to admit. And maybe you have too. I'm inviting you to borrow Jesus' world order. According to Him, the reason you need care is the very reason you have the authority to give care. Uniquely, especially, profoundly. He's given you the gift of dependence here on earth so you can help others understand their ultimate spiritual dependence on Jesus.

Only God can arrange for our hurting to be a part of someone else's wholeness. In His equation I can be as much of a caregiver as a care-receiver, which is a pretty radical thought! I can need healing, but I can also be a vital part of the world's healing. Like Jesus, the original upside-down Chaplain, I can find true wellness in the wounding.

Nothing is more universal than pain. The world shares a story of wounding—like our disconnection from Divine Love, the slow death of dreams, backbreaking disappointment in ourselves and others. But we can also share the story of healing. Healing can happen when we take ownership of our pain, commit to caring for each other, and humble ourselves enough to accept care in return.

I'm learning to hold my own helplessness with compassion and enter into the helplessness of others with the confidence that God is using both the caregivers and care-receivers to heal the world.

If it's true for me, could it be true for you too?

MY HURTING CAN BE A PART OF SOMEONE ELSE'S HEALING.

76

MORE THAN NORMAL

I t'll be just like building with my LEGOs!" John proclaimed as he tore into the cardboard box on my bedroom floor.

He and James had been tasked with assembling, of all things, a bedside toilet. A bedside toilet *for me*, to get specific. While I appreciated John's enthusiasm, I knew this whole situation was bound to become a traumatizing memory that my sons would inevitably have to unpack with an overpriced therapist in about twenty years.

Earlier that week I had taken a terrible fall that left me unable to bear any weight on my right leg. As if the previous years of life with disabilities hadn't killed the remainder of my ego, I had to purchase a bedside toilet in order to avoid risky trips to and from the bathroom. Miraculously, I had somehow managed to avoid this particular medical device up to that point in my poststroke life. But the commode came calling at long last.

When the unassembled toilet arrived in its box, Jay tried mightily to spin this new household addition into a festive game. He tossed the package to the boys and told them to use the instruction pamphlet to put the pieces together as quickly as they could. The boys pounced on the challenge with great delight.

A few feet away, I lay in bed (in tears) and watched my sons assemble the commode. I was overcome with shame. *My kids deserve a normal mom*, I brooded. *A mom who can drive them to soccer practice and bake their birthday cakes and go for a run with them. They deserve so much more than I can give them. Certainly more than a bedside toilet!*

As I continued to watch my boys delight in the epic adventure of building the bedside commode, my shame shifted into a mystifying gratitude. Even in the midst of our collective hardship—my broken leg and our broken lives—my sons were finding joy in the process and deep connection with each other. I thought my boys deserved an ordinary mom. But then I understood they are worth nothing short of an *extraor-dinary* mom who has known extraordinary suffering. The only way my kids will miss out is if I fail to fully embrace the *not normal* mom I actually am.

I can't drive them to school, but I can give them all the wisdom I've earned by the hardest efforts. I can't bike with them, but I can teach them to keep persevering. I can't run with them, but I can show them how to respond with grace and gratitude no matter the circumstances. I can't assemble their swing set, but I can teach them how to build a bedside toilet. (Hey, who knows when it may come in handy?)

The trauma I've experienced could seem like a curse on the people I love, but now I choose to see it as an inheritance of breathtaking value. When intertwined, suffering and hope have the power to change the way we see and live out the rest of our lives. And what better gift could I offer my sons than to live with that kind of perspective?

Friend, you can offer the very same gift to the ones you love. Don't shortchange them by pretending to be anything less than extraordinary. They should be honored to assemble your bedside toilet!

Surviving my suffering means I can offer my kids—and all the people around me—living, breathing proof that life can be hard/good at the same time. I can give people permission to learn to love their lives, even if their futures don't turn out exactly how they expected. With wild generosity, I can share the gifts I've found in the darkness.

If it's true for me, could it be true for you too?

I CAN SEE MY SUFFERING AS A CURSE ON THE PEOPLE I
LOVE OR AS AN INHERITANCE OF BREATHTAKING VALUE.

77

LAVISHING THE GRATITUDE

During a recent train ride in the Atlanta airport, I struck up a conversation with a weary-looking woman donning an airport employee badge on a lanyard around her neck. She told me she had just pushed a passenger in a wheelchair through every single terminal of the sprawling complex because he was afraid of riding the interterminal train. When she'd dropped the passenger off at his gate, the man simply got up and declared, "I made it!" without a single word of thanks, much less a tip. *Yikes.*

As the recipient of many airport wheelchair pushes myself, I was horrified by this story. I whipped out my wallet and tipped the woman with the little cash I had on behalf of her last passenger. By the end of our short ride together, she was sobbing. You better believe she walked away with a copy of my book *Hope Heals* tucked under her arm!

I've decided my mission on earth is to change the emotional thermostat of the Atlanta airport by pulling stunts like this. My goal is lofty, I know, considering it's the world's busiest airport and not exactly renowned for its welcoming atmosphere. But after over two hundred trips in and out of old Hartsfield–Jackson over the last five years, I think I might be making some progress.

No matter how late I am for a flight or the extent of personal space invasion I'm undergoing during the inevitable security pat down (seriously, what do they think I'm smuggling onto these planes?), I intentionally make eye contact and thank anyone I interact with. If an employee is wearing a name tag that I'm able to read, I make a point to call them by their name. More than any other public spaces, airports tempt us to dehumanize one another out of anxiety, frustration, or thoughtlessness. I've challenged myself to do the opposite whenever I can. Even if that challenge is usually inefficient and painfully awkward, no one is safe from my effusive expressions of gratitude.

My goal is not to draw attention to myself. I couldn't be less interested in doing that. Instead, I want to be a living, breathing billboard for hope. Your eyes would have to be as bad as mine to miss the fact that I've been through some hard stuff. My physical disabilities are highly conspicuous, but I want my hope to be just as conspicuous as my hardship. So I lay it on thick. I'm leveraging the pain I wear on the outside to challenge the people around me to overflow with gratitude, patience, and love too. Even when life is really hard. I want to gently remind all of us—and myself—that our pain does not entitle us to treat others carelessly.

My pain has given me a little platform that extends beyond any stages I get to stand (or sit) on. It would be deeply hypocritical for me to travel week after week to spread my hard-won lessons of hope in churches and arenas and auditoriums without being able to share that same hope with the people who get me on the plane in the first place.

I didn't choose my story, and you didn't choose yours. But we can resolve to tap into the benefits of our circumstances, no matter how insignificant they may seem. In my situation, the suffering I've survived gives me a little bit of authority to call others into empathy as they interact with the world. And that's a privilege! No one is going to witness the disabled woman in a wheelchair lavishing her gratitude on every airport employee within earshot without feeling at least slightly inspired to do some lavishing of their own.

Every time my deep hurt can inspire deep hope, my soul heals a little more. I marvel at the way God has brought privilege from my pain.

If it's true for me, could it be true for you too?

THE SUFFERING I'VE SURVIVED GIVES ME
AUTHORITY TO CALL OTHERS INTO EMPATHY.

78

FOR GOOD

I had the strange fortune of being unconscious in the hours after my stroke, float-ing somewhere between life and death. Jay, on the other hand, was fully and excruciatingly awake for every moment of April 21, 2008.

During his sixteen-hour wait for my lifesaving brain surgery to come to an end, Jay located a Gideon Bible in the hospital chapel. At a loss for what to read, he flipped to the eighth chapter of Romans, since it contains one of my all-time favorite passages: "We know that in all things God works for the good of those who love him, who have been called according to his purpose" (v. 28). He read it over and over again until the sun finally rose on April 22. In the soft morning light, my weary neurosurgeon found Jay in the waiting room and delivered the good news. Which also happened to be the bad news. "Katherine lived," the doctor said quietly, "but there will be deficits."

That new day came with new mercies and just as many new unknowns— unknowns we never could have imagined just twenty-four hours before. But even on that morning of mourning, Jay was able to name one good thing that was rippling from the epicenter of our tragedy: *life*.

As I clawed my way from the edge of death over the following months and years, our understanding of Romans 8 would remain in constant tension with our lived experience of suffering. Actively choosing to believe that God was bringing goodness from our pain—as unreasonable as it felt—was the costliest act of faith I could offer. Eventually, that unrelenting investment produced returns. The tireless asking and seeking and knocking on every door in search of the good produced a resilient wonder and robust hope in me. A hope capable of transcending the doubts and the hurts.

Several years into my recovery, Jay and I began sharing our story publicly. Repeatedly telling the story of the worst day of your life can feel cathartic, but it can also make the miracle seem a little rote. You tell a story often enough, and it loses its punch. At some point, we might have become immune to the wonder of all the goodness God had worked out—and was working out—through our suffering. At times, telling our small story may have obscured our view of the bigger story.

We were invited to speak at a small gathering hosted by Jay's sister Sarah and her husband, Jeremiah. As Jay and I wrapped up our well-worn spiel, a young woman in the group asked, "What have been the good things resulting from your worst thing?" We were momentarily taken aback. Not because our experience of goodness through pain wasn't real, but because, even in the midst of the deep knowing, we had forgotten to intentionally see and name and wonder at the good things in front of us and around us.

Jeremiah quietly interjected. "Were it not for Katherine's stroke, Sarah would not have left her two-year missionary post in Africa to care for James. We wouldn't have gotten married when we did, and we certainly wouldn't have had the four kids we have now. Katherine's worst thing gave me most of the good things in my life."

The "good" of Romans 8:28 doesn't erase the hard stuff in my life or in yours. But I have good news—you don't have to pretend that it does. Some shade of the heartbreak and trauma and sadness will remain. You can acknowledge the reality of your pain while also acknowledging the *most real* reality: the good within the pain. Redemption doesn't require eliminating the hard things. Redemption integrates *all* things until a very good whole—a very good *together*—emerges. And that sounds a lot like healing to me.

By inviting me to name the good on that summer evening in my brother-in-law's living room, that young woman called me into a more healed way of living. Every day,

I have the choice to name the good and to marvel at all the "working together" God is doing.

If it's true for me, could it be true for you too?

REDEMPTION DOESN'T REQUIRE ELIMINATING THE HARD THINGS. IT INTEGRATES ALL THINGS UNTIL A VERY GOOD WHOLE EMERGES.

79

MY CLOUD OF WITNESSES

If Corrie ten Boom can survive Ravensbrück, you can get in that water, Katherine!" I sat on the concrete edge of the pool and gently bullied myself to slide into the freezing water for another round of my twice-weekly aquatherapy. After losing half of my cerebellum in the brain surgery that saved my life, I was left with almost no balance or spatial awareness. Layer in substantial muscle loss from months in a hospital bed, and aquatherapy would prove to be the most difficult and dreaded part of my recovery routine.

This is where my (somewhat bizarre) lifelong obsession with Corrie ten Boom became of great use. My beloved childhood hero was an ordinary Dutch woman who helped many Jewish people escape Nazi Germany during World War II. She then survived the horrors of imprisonment in multiple concentration camps. Corrie loved God and lived as a force of hope, no matter the suffering it caused her. So in the strangest hype-up ritual of all time, I invoked the name of Corrie ten Boom whenever I faced therapies or surgeries or tests that I dreaded. In fact, I still do!

Corrie ten Boom is one in an extensive lineup of people in my "cloud of witnesses," as Hebrews 12:1 calls it. The writer described the crowd of veterans who have gone before us, showing us how to live with equal parts strength and softness. These pioneers threw off the doubts, definitions, and distractions that hindered their pursuit of loving and being loved by God. They believed wholeness was ahead of them, and they lived like it—with bright hope and a stubborn commitment to restoration. As I forge ahead in my personal recovery and in my larger healing work in the world, I look to my cloud of witnesses to fuel my endurance every single day.

During those dreaded aquatherapy sessions, my friend Lisa often showed up to watch me. (Yes, this is the same Lisa who inspired me to have my poststroke baby. And yes, she's one heck of a woman!) Lisa had become a quadriplegic literally overnight and lived in the same neurological rehab facility as I did. She couldn't move any of her limbs, so aquatherapy wasn't even an option for her. Even so, she would request to be wheeled to the pool and lowered into the water in a mechanical lift so she could show up to cheer me on during my exercises.

Lisa, I realized, was a part of my cloud of witnesses, even though she was living alongside me then and there. Her very presence pushed me to power through those therapy sessions. And later, the example of Lisa's stubborn creativity within her circumstances would inspire me to share my own story publicly, launch a nonprofit, and even expand our family.

God has provided me with a wealth of witnesses—people I know here and now, and people I will hug for the first time in heaven. People like Lisa and Corrie and my grandmother Manda. Their examples of lives lived with hopeful imagination have been foundational elements in my healing. They are proof that I am not alone on this journey. And neither are you.

I want you to identify your cloud of witnesses, no matter how silly or strange it may feel. Write them down or say their names when you're facing something hard. Study their lives. Validate their suffering and sacrifice by learning from how they lived. As you're carried along by your own cloud of witnesses, figure out how you can become a witness for someone else.

My healing moves forward when a cheering crowd of hope pioneers urges me, "Keep going! There is wholeness ahead." My healing is being made complete when I share that good news with people who need to hear it. By bearing witness to God's work of making all things new, I am being made new too.

If it's true for me, could it be true for you too?

I CAN *LOOK TO* PIONEERS OF HOPE, AND THEN
I CAN *BECOME* A PIONEER OF HOPE.

To be people of faith, living on this side of heaven means constantly stretching ourselves between two wildly different attitudes: we're grateful for what we have now, and still we long for something better ahead. We're left as uncomfortably stretched as Jay Wolf was in the single yoga class we ever took together. The hour crescendoed with Jay arching into the most awe-inspiring "wagon wheel" backbend pose I'd ever seen . . . and then ended in his retirement from yoga. Effective immediately.

The practices of gratitude and anticipation, while equally holy and healthy, seem to be at odds. They pull us in opposite directions between what is and what could be.

But what if this taut space between appreciation and anticipation is actually exactly where hope lives? When put together, gratitude and longing become something more powerful than either practice on its own: an activated expectation, a forward remembrance, a grounded grasping—special kinds of hope that invite us to turn our experiences of personal healing into a longing for universal healing.

My experience of physical healing motivates me to be a part of someone else's soul-level healing. Gratitude for my little family of four stokes a greater yearning to see God graft every person into a place of belovedness. Thankfulness for my warm, safe home makes me long for the day God will draw all people into a space of true belonging. My immense appreciation for a good meal fastens my hopes on the heavenly banquet table where hunger of every kind will be satisfied.

But my thanksgiving cannot dead-end in well-intentioned wishes. It should stir up the momentum of love, justice, and compassion within us. If you and I have been freed for freedom's sake, as Galatians 5:1 tells us, then we've been healed for healing's sake too.

I can be grateful for the goodness of yesterday, *and* I can petition for the betterment of tomorrow, *and* I can take my place in the unfolding redemption story. As Jesus prayed over the fishes and loaves, He gave thanks for God's provision while daring to ask for even more. I, too, can give thanks for what is while straining toward what could be. Contentment can exist without complacency. You might feel like it's an impossible balance to strike. But it gets easier over time, I promise. Like a super-impressive wheel pose.

This may always feel like a stretch for me, but I can accept God's invitation to be a holder of hope within the time and place He's assigned me. I'll hold it with both gratitude and longing, contentment and disruption, grace and grasping for the gifts I've been given and for the goodness we've been promised.

If it's true for me, could it be true for you too?

I CAN GIVE THANKS FOR WHAT *IS* WHILE STRAINING TOWARD WHAT *COULD BE*. CONTENTMENT CAN EXIST WITHOUT COMPLACENCY.

81

WITH-NESS

A wild thing happens after you survive a near-death experience: everyone assumes you are now enlightened, an *ohmm*-ing guru who knows the perfect bits of wisdom to dispense to people in their times of suffering. Like some sort of Jesus-y fortune cookie. No one seems to have caught on to the fact that my ministry manual has not yet arrived in the mail. As of this writing, I don't know much more than any of you do!

For a decade and a half now, I've stood in front of a full-blast fire hydrant of tragic stories from others. The channels through which I receive these tender dispatches seem to multiply by the day—emails, phone calls, handwritten letters, direct messages, texts, skywriting, carrier pigeons, being recognized and flagged down across crowded public spaces to share in the story of a stranger's suffering. I count it a weighty and precious privilege to be trusted with these vulnerable cries for comfort, though I usually feel decidedly un-guru-like.

Since my stroke, I've also been on the receiving end of a lot of well-meaning Bible verse recitations, rhyming platitudes, and conveniently alliterative "truths" about how God never gives us more than we can handle. About how everything happens for a reason. (Maybe you have too, so no spoiler alert needed on my response to those words: Nope. And *big* nope!)

Not one of those comments has ever helped me, and they certainly haven't healed me, although I know every person who said them offered them in love. But I have discovered the single foolproof response to someone else's pain: just show up. Literally, physically, actually put your body in the same rooms as theirs if at all possible.

The great comfort of the Christian tradition is the incarnation of Christ among us in the person of Jesus. The Bible even calls Him by a name that means "God with us." Not "God over us" or "God kinda nearby us." Incarnation—showing up in the flesh—is the final word in solidarity. *Compassion*, after all, means "suffering with."

The first forty days of my poststroke life were spent bound by a rope of monitoring wires to a bed in the intensive care unit. In a waiting room seven floors below, my friends and family set up camp in a corner (or rather Katherine's Korner, as they sweetly named it). Those people showed up day after day to bring trays of hot food, divert Jay with stories, and bounce my baby on their laps. Sometimes they simply sat in silence as living, breathing, flesh-bound proof of God's presence with us through each other.

Jesus isn't repelled by our collective suffering or sadness. His physical presence in our reality is the undeniable proof that we are loved, that we are not alone. The ultimate result of His relentless "with-ness" was, and continues to be, the healing of the world.

Showing the world the with-ness of Jesus can be awkward and maybe even intimidating. But fortunately, it requires no special eloquence or experience, which means we can all be a part of the healing process. Healing happens when we commit to showing up, not just extending feelings of sympathy that inevitably fade. Healing happens when we weep with those who weep, rather than preach at those who grieve. Healing happens when we see a hurting person as a human in need of hope rather than as a problem to be solved.

I was healed—and am still being healed—by the ones who've shown up. So I'm gonna show up too.

If it's true for me, could it be true for you too?

HEALING HAPPENS WHEN WE WEEP WITH THOSE WHO WEEP, RATHER THAN PREACH AT THOSE WHO GRIEVE.

82

COMPASSION FOR
THE CROWD

Somehow, I stumbled into a professional speaking career. Laughably (inexplicably, even!), organizations and churches pay me actual American dollars to show up on their stages and pages to tell the story of a second-chance life born from suffering. This whole situation feels like both a privilege and a punch line, and it puts me in proximity to a whole lot of people.

You can find me in airports what feels like a thousand times a month en route to crowded sanctuaries, conference centers, and even arenas. After many of my speaking engagements, I'm released into the crowd to sign books and hear stories and clasp hands with amazing people who, in partnership with God, have given me a platform. But when you have severe double vision and a deaf ear and balance issues like I do, navigating a crowd is overwhelming and even off-putting at times. I have to hype myself up for the sensory overload of echoing voices displaced by my one-sided hearing and the blur of faces duplicated by my out-of-sync eyes.

But braving the crush of humanity is always, always worth it to me. Surviving to see the other side of suffering changed my physical vision forever, yes. But it also changed the way I look at people. Now, I can see *into* them. I never see past them.

After enduring a life-changing medical crisis, I could have decided I'd spend the rest of my days in a dark corner, convinced that no one would ever understand the mortification I've faced. Speaking from experience, I could live a pretty satisfying life holed up in my bedroom. I do keep snacks in the nightstand, after all!

Blessedly, suffering has had the very opposite effect. It's become a point of connection—and thus, compassion—rather than comparison. Instead of making me feel misunderstood by other people, it's allowed me to understand other people better. My own pain has made the pain of others so much more real. So real that I can feel it in my chest as I roll through crowded airports or hotel lobbies. I don't need to know what they've seen or experienced to know they need compassion as much as I do.

The blur of faces is no longer an obstacle but an invitation to empathy. Every single body rushing past me holds a soul as heavy with joy and fear and bad news and heartache as my own. Being in the middle of the crush reminds me of the tender care we owe each other—whether stranger, sister, or spouse.

Compassion might just be the most valuable treasure I have found in the darkness. In fact, I wouldn't trade it for anything. My friend, if your suffering is still pushing you inward instead of outward, I am praying with my whole heart that God is quick to connect the dots between your pain and other people. Because the network is so very rich.

These days, I feel a tingle of excitement when I roll into those crowded airport terminals and conference center lobbies. I can't wait to look at my fellow busted-up image bearers and bless them in the battles they're fighting. I pray their pain, like mine, becomes a portal into the tender interiors of the people around them. I pray it softens their hearts to the hard stories unfolding everywhere they look. Most of all, I pray they find friendship with the God who chose suffering for the chance to be closer to the crush of humanity.

As I move through the crowds of God's beloved people, I am so grateful that the experience of my own pain compels me toward compassion instead of closing me in to self-preservation.

If it's true for me, could it be true for you too?

MY PAIN CAN COMPEL ME TOWARD COMPASSION
RATHER THAN SELF-PRESERVATION.

83

THE COMMUNION OF COMMON THINGS

One Sunday morning in the early winter months of 2021, our family of four piled into bed to "go" to church. Just a year before, we never could have imagined that church would look like this. Thanks to an alarming surge in COVID-19 cases and a leg injury that had rendered me immobile, our weekly worship service was streamed from a laptop and enjoyed under a ridiculous number of duvets. These homebodies were living their best lives.

That particular morning, the live-streamed service concluded with Communion. On-screen, our pastor stood behind a table set with a hunk of bread and a silver cup. We wanted to participate, too, so we paused the stream and sent our sons downstairs to hunt for Communion elements (or at least Communion-ish elements) in the kitchen.

Apparently, our refrigerator and pantry were bare, and the tumbleweeds rolling around inside them didn't sound too appetizing to James and John. The kids resorted to raiding my supplements cabinet, which, admittedly, is never bare because I love brewing up a wellness potion to sneak into the boys' smoothies. There they dug up an old bottle of multivitamin gummies.

We doled out two gummies for each of us and resumed the live stream. As our pastor recounted Jesus' words at the last shared meal before His death, we popped the gummies into our mouths. And you know what? The remembrance of Christ's broken body and shed blood was just as poignant to me from our overcrowded bed as it's been in any church. There, I said it.

As the service wrapped up, I was reminded of another holy experience *of* church that didn't happen *in* church. Hours after my stroke, when I was still in the surgery that would save my life, dozens of friends from our Bel Air Church Sunday school class descended upon the hospital waiting room. They came with food and hugs and tears, then stayed all night to sing and pray and laugh with Jay in the darkest hours of his life. Obviously, I wasn't present at the gathering, but Jay still describes that night as the most real, most sacred experience of church he has ever encountered.

I love going to church! In fact, I emphatically endorse it. The very first Sunday morning after we moved to Los Angeles as newly married twenty-two-year-olds, we took my father-in-law's advice and got ourselves to a church. (Is it painfully obvious that we are a couple of people-pleasing firstborns?) That's the very church we would attend and serve within for the next fourteen years. God used that place and those people to sustain us in the thick of our suffering.

But if life with disability and a pandemic have taught me anything, it's that I can't depend on the predictable rhythms of church—or health or community or general stability—to put me in a posture of worship, remembrance, and gratitude. And neither can you. Rather, we have to get really good at sifting through our circumstances to find what's sacred. You and I could see our unpredictable, imperfect, and often painful lives as a barrier to deep communion with God. Or we could accept His invitation to find holiness and healing right in the middle of the mess . . . or at the bottom of a bottle of gummy vitamins.

Jesus can be found in all our ordinariness. He's stashed the sacred all around us. He delights in our attempts to commune with Him, however humble they may be. I'm learning to feast on the communion of common things to experience Christ's uncommon power in this moment, and the next, and the next.

If it's true for me, could it be true for you too?

COMMUNION WITH CHRIST IS ALWAYS AVAILABLE TO ME, EVEN IN THE COMMONPLACE.

84

EXPANSION

Four grueling years of grief and grit finally gave way to a summer brimming with promise and beauty. In 2012, for the first time since my stroke, life felt manageable and a new kind of normalcy seemed within reach. Jay and I had lined up a dizzying agenda of family travel plans and even secured our first paid speaking engagement. James would begin kindergarten in the fall, and I was making fabulous progress toward my therapy goal of walking with him on the one-block journey to school.

At long last, we were coming back to life.

And then halfway through July, I fell and broke my leg during a visit to my parents' house. In an instant, our maxed-out summer calendar was wiped empty. Unable to fly, I took up semipermanent residence in a rented hospital bed in the middle of my parents' living room. At my firm insistence, Jay flew across the country to take on our speaking engagement solo.

For a brief moment, I thought the world was stretching out before me in bright expanses of possibility and hope. Just as I began peering up from the deep, dark hole of four years of suffering, the loud *crack* of a broken leg startled me back into a self-protective huddle. I felt like a fool for believing life could be good again. Raise your hand if you've ever been victimized by your own optimism.

We eventually returned to California, and summer gave way to fall. On James's first day of kindergarten, I made the one-block journey to his school in a wheelchair, my physical therapy goals to walk him there made irrelevant by my broken leg. I would spend months grappling with the implicit expectation that my recovery would be a linear, upward trajectory—a notion I hadn't even realized I'd believed until it was proven to be untrue. Somewhere in your heart of hearts, I bet you've believed this too.

The following winter was unusually cold for California. Our world shrank to the size of our little yellow house. With no heat in our home, Jay, James, and I made a habit of piling into bed for warmth and watching an irresponsible amount of mindless TV. In those days of depression and dormancy, we quietly searched our hearts and minds for what God might have us do with our lives (and livelihoods) within these unstable, unreliable circumstances.

Reckoning with our lifelong assignment of cyclical wounding and healing proved to be the ultimate reality check in the most hurtful and helpful of ways. Slowly, Jay and I realized that we wouldn't be released from the cycle on this side of heaven, and neither would anyone else. So we might as well learn to live within it. Not only live but thrive. And maybe we could help others do the same.

Our realization turned to resolve. In one of the emptiest seasons of our lives, we finally found the space to begin building the foundations of what would become our full-time ministry. Slowly and tentatively, we raised our heads up from our huddle of pain to look into a future that might just hold good things.

At some point, each of us will realize that there's no escaping the cycle of wounding and healing. We can resist it, or we can lean into it. Expect it. Evolve with it.

If pain shrinks us, hope expands us. When I live with hope, suffering doesn't have to shut me down. Instead, it has the potential to be my deepest source of empathy, strongest point of connection, and most convincing reason for change. Expansion is not comfortable, and neither is hope. It has stretched and strained me. But, above all, it has saved me.

If it's true for me, could it be true for you too?

SUFFERING CAN BE A SOURCE OF EMPATHY, POINT OF CONNECTION, AND MOTIVATION FOR GROWTH.

85

THE WHOLE BLASTED, BLESSED PROCESS

There's definitely something wrong with your brain."

I've sat across the desks of dozens of doctors throughout my poststroke tenure. One doctor in particular remains forever distinguished in my memory as the physician with the worst bedside manner of all time. It was almost impressive, honestly. I would call him zany, but that may lead you to believe something about him was endearing. It was not.

Right there in the geneticist's office, I felt a frustrated scream-cry forcing its way upward from deep in my chest. I spent every bit of my self-control shoving it down. I'd lived through an AVM rupture, an aneurysm coiling, and multiple vertebral dissections, only to be told that "all was not well" inside my knotted-up brain.

I panicked. *This cannot be my story. This cannot be my life. I thought I'd gotten to the healing part of this whole deal. But maybe the suffering has only just begun.*

For a long time I wanted to believe the narrative that said I was a stroke survivor, the one that put my pain in the past tense. In part, that story is true and deeply good. But the full scope of my situation is much more complex. The truth is the hardest parts of my life on earth are probably ahead of me. I have a lifelong, ongoing neurovascular disorder so uncommon that it doesn't even have a name. People with this disorder are rarely identified because almost none of us live long enough to be diagnosed. For some reason I have been allowed to survive the unsurvivable, again and again and again. But one day I won't survive.

As awareness of my unnamed neurovascular condition slowly turns into acceptance, I'm inviting God to help me make sense of this new reality. *When this condition finally takes me down*, I often find myself wondering, *will my story still be called good? Will my hope be put to shame if I don't survive?*

A low, gentle voice answers my question with a question. *Since when has hope been about surviving, Katherine?*

Whether I acknowledged it or not, hope had been a destination to me. Something to be attained or achieved. I thought I could successfully complete a one-time progressive ascent from hurting to healing to hoping, then hang out at the top for the rest of my life. Easy breezy! Maybe this sounds like something you've believed too.

It turns out what I thought was a one-way ascent is actually a cycle, an endless tumbling of hurting into healing into hoping into hurting—and on and on it goes. I'd been mistaken for a long time. Hope is not a fixed point we can reach. Hope is the living force that propels us through the rest of the blasted, blessed process of hurting and healing. And as the cycle progresses, so does hope. It evolves and expands and deepens. Over a lifetime, I think our hope will take as many forms as our hurts do. At the end of all the tumbling, I think hope will carry us to the place where we won't need it anymore.

As long as we live, you and I will continue to sit across desks from tone-deaf doctors who make us want to scream. We'll keep taking tumbles that hurt our hearts even more than they hurt our bodies. We will lose things we didn't even realize we could lose. The cycle will continue. But hear me, dear one. If we are propelled by an ever-deepening hope, we can keep hurting and healing in the right direction. We don't have to be afraid of or surprised by a spiral.

I'm surrendering to the age-old rhythm of being wounded so I can be healed, then being healed enough to hope that good things are ahead. Then, stronger yet softer than I was before, I'll be thrown into the cycle again, ready to face all the fresh hurts awaiting those of us who survive long enough to suffer again.

If it's true for me, could it be true for you too?

HOPE IS NOT A FIXED POINT I WILL REACH. HOPE IS THE LIVING FORCE THAT PROPELS ME THROUGH THE ONGOING CYCLE OF HURTING AND HEALING.

8 6

WOUNDED HEALERS

S uffering people have an uncanny knack for finding me. I must have some sort of scent. Almost daily, a desperate friend or family member of a person in crisis will track down an acquaintance who reaches out to a neighbor who knows my fourth cousin twice removed all in the hopes of getting in touch with me.

For years this scrambling for comfort terrified me. I felt unequipped for the task of meeting these gaping needs with hope. My spiritual shoulders sagged under the weight of my ever-growing awareness of suffering in the world.

Every last one of my encounters with strangers in pain claims a permanent place in my heart. I will never forget how violently my hands shook as I dialed the number of a woman who was scheduled to have her leg amputated the next morning. As we both wept on the call, a beautiful transfer of courage took place. She borrowed some of my bravery.

I remember sitting at my kitchen table with a couple who told me, through tears, about three decades of caring for their daughter. A rare genetic disorder had reduced her to near physical and cognitive infancy in her final years. Her aging parents were experiencing nothing short of PTSD and had found themselves in my kitchen in their search for hope after her death.

Two young parents called me from a hospital room as they were making the decision to turn off life support for their daughter, who had fallen off a golf cart and sustained total brain damage. They wanted guidance, so they tracked me down.

I carry every one of these stories—and thousands more—somewhere deep in my soul. I will never stop hurting for the hurting. There was a time when these exchanges felt excruciating and gut-wrenching. My stomach would ache for days afterward.

But after a while, I realized that entering into other people's suffering could actually be a part of my healing. A really, really important part. These invitations into the pain of other people have become sacred. I'm not scared of them anymore. Since I have received the overwhelming comfort and generous empathy of so many friends and strangers, how can I withhold comfort from people who need it?

In a million creative ways, God has comforted you and me during our journeys into the darkness. He has given us His Spirit, His Word, and His people. But He never intended us to be reservoirs, damming all that goodness up. God comforts us so we can comfort other people (2 Corinthians 1:4–5). He uses our suffering to give us the authority—like a set of credentials—to show up for other people in their times of crisis. In return, their need for comfort redeems our own suffering in some small way. And one day, the recipients of our comfort will go and do likewise in a beautiful cycle of mutual ministry in which nothing is wasted.

Beloved, longing for redemption is the most natural response to suffering we can have. God tucked a need for restoration into our DNA. If you're on the lookout for redemption in your story, seek out someone who is suffering today. Opt into God's perfectly designed plan for healing. Show up with those hard-won credentials and shed some tears. Convince those hurting people that they are not alone. Once you're able to offer true-blue empathy, your pain is put to use. It's redeemed, if only a little. And you are healed, if only a little.

While I no longer fear entering into the suffering of others, I am deeply afraid of fatiguing my capacity for compassion and missing my opportunities for healing. Every day I ask God to thicken my skin as He softens my heart, to teach me to empathize but not internalize. These are the prayers of a wounded healer. Comforted to comfort. Redeemed to redeem.

If it's true for me, could it be true for you too?

WHEN I COMFORT OTHER PEOPLE, MY SUFFERING
CAN BE REDEEMED, BIT BY BIT.

87

SHIFTING PERSPECTIVE

The scene before me looked nearly apocalyptic. The stuffy hospital hallway, lit by blinking fluorescent lights, was lined with rollaway beds and stretchers as far as I could see. Every one of them was occupied by someone sick or injured or desperate enough to come to the emergency room in the middle of a pandemic. Including myself.

For the first time in over twelve years, I was at the hospital alone. I'd taken a terrible fall that afternoon and my knee needed immediate medical attention. Jay, who had been by my side at every doctor's appointment and ER visit and hospital stay since my stroke, hadn't been allowed to accompany me past the front entrance per the hospital's COVID-19 policies. (For the record, he did not go down without a fight . . . and the fight was kind of glorious.)

As I sat on my assigned stretcher in that heinous hallway, I felt pretty sorry for myself. But it didn't take long for the pity party to shift into a new perspective as I looked at the other patients all around me. Because of the masking and social distancing protocols, I wasn't able to strike up any conversations. However, I didn't need to exchange any words with these folks to understand their stories. A glance into their scared, tired eyes told me all I needed to know.

I would be in that hallway for almost twelve hours, and I used most of that time thinking about the millions of patients around the world who were facing their hardest days all alone. About the single parents who had no backup plan when they were unwell. About people with disabilities who wouldn't be caught by the safety net of a loving community when life dropped them into a free fall. About elderly folks who had outlived their family and friends. Meanwhile, I would return home to a capable caregiver, an accessible home, a mile of meal trains, and school carpool offers for months. The good fortune of my situation was almost shameful.

Perspective can lead to shame for the stories God has given us, especially when those stories feel so much "better" than someone else's. Or maybe we feel shame because we're stuck in a bad situation that we feel like we should have been able to prevent. *If only I'd shown up for other people, they'd be showing up for me,* you may find yourself thinking. Either way, no shame is good shame, no matter what it's about. Shame undermines God's goodness to us and renders us less effective in our work toward healing. If anyone is capable of producing shame out of thin air—much less out of honest ingredients—it's me. I speak with authority when I say it's a total waste of time. Zero stars. Would not recommend.

From that hospital stretcher, I prayed for the people for whom my heart broke. I prayed for people by name, and I prayed for people who were only hypothetical. I prayed for healing to happen in the ways they needed it most—maybe physically, maybe otherwise. Most of all, I prayed that those people could access a hope that would carry them through the thick of their suffering. When my heart wanted to shrink in on itself, I fought for it to expand instead.

Shame can force us into pity or self-protection, or it can invite us into compassion and action. Our hearts don't have to harden after we are hurt, and we certainly don't have to feel shame as they heal. When our hearts shatter, it's possible for them to be put back together again, more tender to other people's pain than ever before. But we can't let the hard shell of shame get in the way of the mending.

When we choose hope instead of shame, our healed hearts can help heal the world. And if that kind of heart can be formed from suffering, then I'm willing to wake up tomorrow to persevere through more of it.

If it's true for me, could it be true for you too?

MY HEART DOESN'T HAVE TO HARDEN AFTER I AM HURT. WHEN MY HEART SHATTERS, IT CAN BE PUT BACK TOGETHER IN A FORM MORE TENDER TO OTHERS' PAIN.

88

DANCING IN THE HOUSE
OF MOURNING

L et me get this straight. You end the last night of camp with a *dance*?" I asked. My poker face has never been strong, and I was begging my expression to stay neutral. It was 2014. Jay and I had just arrived at a weeklong retreat for families with disabilities where we'd been hired to speak, and I was meeting with the retreat director to get all the details for the week.

"Yes! It's the best hour of the entire week. Everyone gets really into it!" she answered without a trace of irony. In a PTSD-like flashback, I imagined the dimly lit gyms of my early teen years. Sweaty crowds of my classmates dropped it low to the biggest hits of the mid-1990s during our quarterly school dances. Meanwhile I hung close to the security of the snack table. Then my brain superimposed people with disabilities onto the scene. I shuddered. I couldn't imagine anything less dignifying for me or these folks I'd come to love!

Even with this nerve-racking finale in the back of our minds, Jay and I dove into the retreat festivities. We enjoyed every minute with an audience of our disabled peers and their caregivers—all of whom had become dear new friends. The end of the week arrived, and after our final dinner together, all the campers migrated over to an outdoor pavilion overlooking a lake. A speaker system was fired up, glow sticks were distributed, and every person in the crowd boogied for the next hour. People in wheelchairs, grandmas, toddlers, too-cool teenagers, kids with intellectual disabilities, nonverbal campers, men and women with terminal diagnoses all danced with total joy and abandon. It was the weirdest, most wonderful sixty minutes of my life.

Just a few years later, we "inherited" that retreat and formed the scaffolding of Hope Heals Camp. As we adjusted and updated some features of the retreat to make it our own, I emphatically insisted that the dance party stay in the program. I've lost count of how many Hope Heals Camp dance parties I've boogied at in the years since, but the magic has yet to wear off.

There's a sort of strange verse in Ecclesiastes (7:2) that says we're better off in the house of mourning than the house of feasting, that we have more to learn from a funeral than a wedding since we're all headed to the grave. I think you could learn the wrong lesson from that verse and start living as if being somber or sad is a virtue. But if you've been to a Hope Heals Camp dance party, then you've peeked inside a house of mourning full of people who have known death in many forms. It's not a sad or somber place. In fact, a radical freedom buzzes in the air that's only possible among people who understand that life—in all its horror and beauty—is temporary. That it's to be held with open hands. We dance together in the altogether absence of self-consciousness that only develops once you stop relying on ability, strength, or certainty to make you happy.

King David famously credited God with turning his wailing into dancing (Psalm 30:11). I'm beginning to understand that doesn't mean God made the mourning vanish. Instead, maybe God just made mourning a part of the dance.

Dear one, has your suffering set you free? Or has it bound you up in fear or shame? I'm extending a hand to you to follow me onto God's version of the dance floor. Here, the music swells with high notes and low notes, major chords and minor chords. The crowd is gracious because they've been exactly where you've been. And they live in joyful anticipation of the most real party that's to come once we leave the house of mourning for good.

For me, sitting in the house of mourning has disrupted the myth that life is good only when I am secure or able or in control. So now I can just dance with all the other mourners who have been set free, just like I have.

If it's true for me, could it be true for you too?

SUFFERING CAN SET ME FREE TO UNDERSTAND THAT LIFE—
IN ALL ITS HORROR AND BEAUTY—IS TEMPORARY.

89

PRACTICING HEAVEN

When I was growing up, heaven was a place called summer camp. As I've already told you more than once, each June and July of my childhood and adolescent years, I spent eight perfect weeks in a magical place called Camp DeSoto, situated in northern Alabama along the Highway above the Clouds. (Yes, that's the real address!) It is a place of simplicity, wonder, and that boundless kind of freedom only children can access. I internalized God's goodness there. I previewed the pure delight He intends for me in this life and the next.

Simply put, when I was at camp, I knew I belonged.

My senior year, I wrapped up my tenure at Camp DeSoto on a skyscraping high. I, Katherine Wolf, was chosen to be the chief of the Chickasaw Tribe. Yes, *the* Chickasaw Tribe of the 1999 DeSoto Final Cup fame. (Remember the best day of my life?!) So naturally, after my freshman year of college, I eagerly returned to Camp DeSoto to serve as a counselor. I was so excited about my new role in this little slice of heaven.

As the following summers came and went—college, then married life, then parenthood—DeSoto drifted from the rhythms of my adulthood. However, a new kind of camp would find its way into my poststroke life through the most unexpected means when Jay and I took over that existing disability family camp in 2017. And of all places, that camp was located in northern Alabama. In the summers since, Hope Heals Camp has offered life-changing (and lifesaving) relationships and spiritual resources to families experiencing all kinds of disabilities and heartaches.

Hope Heals Camp has been described in a lot of wonderful ways over the years. As a thin place between earth and eternity. The upside-down kingdom embodied.

The most real reality. A joyful rebellion. Last summer, our psychiatrist friend Dr. Curt Thompson joined us as a camp pastor. Curt has an uncanny knack for wrapping exactly the right words around indescribable experiences. As his week at camp came to a close, he told us it felt like we had been "practicing heaven together." (Whew. Write my eulogy, Curt!)

Turns out, childhood Katherine was onto something. Heaven does look like a summer camp. But the summer camp I see now isn't one of childhood innocence or boundless freedom or intact dreams of a promising future. It's a community of people who have been redefined by suffering. It's a place full of pain but free from pretense.

At its core, it's an experience of near-total belonging and belovedness. That experience isn't exclusive to Hope Heals Camp. As we wait for the real deal, you and I can practice heaven day in and day out, in the middle of our imperfect lives. We can put ourselves in the presence of truly free people. We can name the good in our hard days because now we know God's not withholding it. We can sing as we cry and dance as we mourn. We can keep fighting to believe we are fully known and fully loved by God exactly as we are, and treat others like they are known and loved too. How are you going to practice heaven today?

To me, the simplest definition of *heaven* is being where God is. Which means I can participate in heaven right here and right now. I practice heaven when I recognize how God is showing up in every person, every place, and every pain. I don't have to wait for my body to be cured or my tears to be wiped away or my questions to be answered. I can delight in God's presence in the present. As I patiently wait for the fullest experience of being face-to-face with Divine Love itself, I can catch glimpses right where I am.

If it's true for me, could it be true for you too?

I PRACTICE HEAVEN WHEN I COMMIT TO RECOGNIZING HOW GOD IS SHOWING UP IN EVERY PERSON, EVERY PLACE, AND EVERY PAIN.

90

A BENEDICTION FOR THE
GOOD/HARD LIFE

When I was recently offered the opportunity to speak to a stadium full of college-aged students at a massive New Year's conference, I felt precisely as excited as I felt intimidated . . . and kind of nauseated. As I started to work on what I would say, I somehow convinced myself that it was up to me, Katherine Wolf, to deliver *the* message that would galvanize a generation. To be clear, no one had told me this was the case. But I always work best under pressure.

The first step in writing the speech that would change the world was procrastinating. Like, a lot. (Hey, don't judge my process.) But in all those days and weeks of *not* technically writing my message, I did spend a lot of time thinking about those who would hear the message. A stadium full of young hearts and minds—not to mention the much larger live-stream audience—poised on the front edge of their God-given good/hard. A generation being told from every conceivable source that avoiding pain is the goal, rather than seeking true abundance.

My chest ached and my eyes filled with tears as I thought of the suffering that would seep into the lives of every one of these precious young people. As I prayerfully held them in the embrace of my imagination, I also found a younger version of myself held there too. The version who had no idea what beautiful and terrible things were to come for her. My instinct was to wrap my arms around them, to shield them—and myself—from all the brokenness. Of course, I knew I could never really protect them. I sure as heck couldn't prevent any of the pain. But I knew I could help prepare them.

It didn't take long for the words to pour out of me.

I want to share some of those words with you today. But, dear one, if you've arrived at the final pages of this book, I know you don't need a spoiler alert about suffering. No one needs to tell you that life will be hard. You've seen it and tasted it. And, so far, you've survived it. Which is exactly why I'm not sharing these words in the form of instructions or platitudes. I'm speaking them over you as a prayer. I pray them over myself too.

I hope you can return to these words again and again to remember that there will be treasures in the darkest parts of your life. I hope you'll borrow these words for yourself and for the people you love. Mostly, I hope these words will help you love your one-and-only life enough to live it well until the very end.

This is for you. A benediction for the good/hard life.

May you see your life as a good/hard story that God is writing (Psalm 139:16).
May you open your hands to release old dreams and receive new ones (Isaiah 43:18–19).
May you find the miracle you've been looking for has been right in front of you all along (John 12:37).
May you accept the stunning capacity you have to endure because of Jesus, who endured for you (John 16:33).
May you live out the hardest parts of your life with a joyful rebellion against the darkness (Deuteronomy 31:6).
May you believe that the boundaries around your life are good and pleasant because God uniquely assigned them to you (Psalm 16:6).
May your invisible wheelchairs become avenues to a new kind of freedom because of Jesus (Hebrews 4:15).

I CAN'T PREVENT ALL PAIN OR FULLY PROTECT MYSELF
FROM IT. BUT I CAN RESOLVE TO ENDURE IT WELL.

DO YOU WANT THE *GIFTS*,

OR DO YOU WANT THE

GIVER HIMSELF?

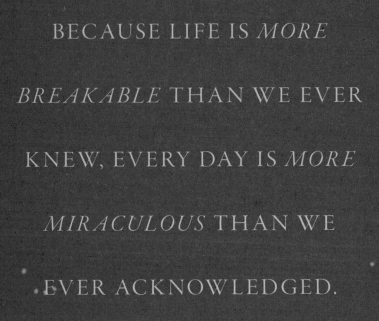

BECAUSE LIFE IS *MORE*

BREAKABLE THAN WE EVER

KNEW, EVERY DAY IS *MORE*

MIRACULOUS THAN WE

EVER ACKNOWLEDGED.

EVERY *HARD DAY*

OF YOUR LIFE HAS

PREPARED YOU FOR

THE *HARDEST DAY*

OF YOUR LIFE.

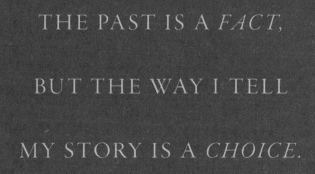

THE PAST IS A *FACT*,

BUT THE WAY I TELL

MY STORY IS A *CHOICE*.

CELEBRATION CAN

BE A FORM OF WORSHIP,

A *JOYFUL REBELLION* AGAINST

FEAR AND DESPAIR.

GOD PREFERS TO WORK

WITHIN LIMITATIONS BECAUSE

THOSE LIMITATIONS PROVE

JUST HOW *UNSTOPPABLE*

HIS POWER IS.

BROKENNESS CAN LEAD

TO A *KIND OF HEALING*

THAT MAKES US *MORE WHOLE*

THAN WE EVER WERE BEFORE

THE BREAKING.

WHAT IS *TRUE*

IN THE LIGHT IS STILL

TRUE IN THE DARK.

THE *BEST FRUIT* IN MY

LIFE GREW FROM THE SOIL

OF MY *WORST MOMENTS.*

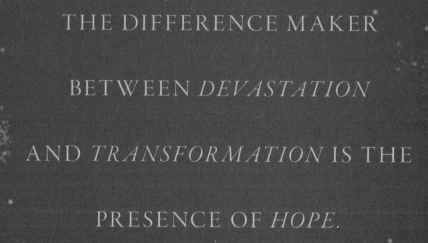

THE DIFFERENCE MAKER

BETWEEN *DEVASTATION*

AND *TRANSFORMATION* IS THE

PRESENCE OF *HOPE*.

SUFFERING CAN FEEL

MORE BEARABLE WHEN

WE LIKE WHO WE'VE BECOME

BECAUSE OF IT.

IF PAIN *SHRINKS* US,

HOPE *EXPANDS* US.

JESUS *REPURPOSES*

OUR PAIN AS THE BUILDING

BLOCKS OF *REDEMPTION.*

MAYBE THE TRUEST,

STRONGEST *YOU* IS WAITING

ON THE OTHER SIDE OF

THE *BREAKING.*

A *GOOD LIFE* WAS WAITING

FOR ME WHEN I WAS

WILLING TO *REDEFINE* WHAT

GOODNESS REALLY WAS.

NOTES

1. Sir Richard Baker, "Meditations Upon the LXXXIV Psalme of David," *Meditations and Disquisitions, Upon the Seven Consolatorie Psalmes of David* (London: I. Dawson, 1640; Ann Arbor, MI: Text Creation Partnership, 2011), 140–141, http://name.umdl.umich.edu/A02119.0001.001.

2. There is no evidence to date that Spurgeon said this exactly. Rather, the quote appears to be based on a sermon Spurgeon gave in 1874, titled "Sin and Grace": "The wave of temptation may even wash you higher up upon the Rock of ages, so that you cling to it with a firmer grip than you have ever done before." See Staff, "6 Things Spurgeon Didn't Say," blog, The Spurgeon Center, August 24, 2016, www.spurgeon.org/resource-library/blog-entries/6-things-spurgeon-didnt-say/.

3. Jodi Page, "Fear Not, for I Have Redeemed You," by Jodi Page, ©1975 Celebration/Kingsway's Music.

4. Global Health Estimates: *Leading Causes of Death*, The Global Health Observatory, World Health Organization, quoted in "The Top 10 Causes of Death," World Health Organization, December 9, 2020, https://www.who.int /news-room/fact-sheets/detail/the-top-10-causes-of-death.

5. "Manifesto: The Mad Farmer Liberation Front," in Wendell Berry, *The Country of Marriage* (New York: Harcourt Brace Jovanovich, 1973). Also published by Counterpoint Press in *The Selected Poems of Wendell Berry*, 1999; *The Mad Farmer Poems*, 2008; and *New Collected Poems*, 2012.

ABOUT THE AUTHORS

KATHERINE WOLF is a survivor and advocate who leverages her redemptive story to encourage those with broken bodies, broken brains, and broken hearts. She and her husband, Jay, have coauthored two books, *Hope Heals* and *Suffer Strong*. In 2017, they founded Hope Heals Camp, an intergenerational retreat experience for families with disabilities. In 2023, they opened Mend Coffee & Goods, a community hub offering dignifying employment to adults with disabilities in a beautiful, universally designed space for customers of all abilities. Katherine and Jay live in Atlanta with their two sons.

ALEX WOLF is the experience and content director at Hope Heals, where she has the honor of creating inclusive spaces and communities for families affected by disabilities. She also has directed Hope Heals Camp since its founding in 2017. It is the joy of her life. Alex and her husband, Henry (the other joy of her life), live in Birmingham, Alabama.